180 Days of Social-Emotional Learning

for Fifth Grade

Kayse Hinrichsen, M.A.

Consultant

Kris Hinrichsen, M.A.T., NBCT
Teacher and Educational Consultant
Anchorage School District

Amy Zoque
Teacher and Instructional Coach
Ontario Montclair School District

Publishing Credits

Corinne Burton, M.A.Ed., *Publisher*
Emily R. Smith, M.A.Ed., *VP of Content Development*
Lynette Ordoñez, *Content Specialist*
David Slayton, *Assistant Editor*
Jill Malcolm, *Multimedia Specialist*

Image Credits: all images from iStock and/or Shutterstock

Social-Emotional Learning Framework

The CASEL SEL framework and competencies were used in the development of this series.
© 2020 The Collaborative for Academic, Social, and Emotional Learning

A division of Teacher Created Materials
5482 Argosy Avenue
Huntington Beach, CA 92649-1039
www.tcmpub.com/shell-education
ISBN 978-1-0876-4974-0
© 2022 Shell Educational Publishing, Inc

Table of Contents

Introduction

"SEL is the process through which all young people and adults acquire and apply the knowledge, skills, and attitudes to develop healthy identities, manage emotions and achieve personal and collective goals, feel and show empathy for others, establish and maintain supportive relationships, and make responsible and caring decisions." (CASEL 2020)

Social-emotional learning (SEL) covers a wide range of skills that help people improve themselves and get fulfilment from their relationships. They are the skills that help propel us into the people we want to be. SEL skills give people the tools to think about the future and manage the day-to-day goal setting to get where we want to be.

The National Commission for Social, Emotional, and Academic Development (2018) noted that children need many skills, attitudes, and values to succeed in school, future careers, and life. "They require skills such as paying attention, setting goals, collaboration and planning for the future. They require attitudes such as internal motivation, perseverance, and a sense of purpose. They require values such as responsibility, honesty, and integrity. They require the abilities to think critically, consider different views, and problem solve." Explicit SEL instruction will help students develop and hone these important skills, attitudes, and values.

Daniel Goleman (2005), a social scientist who popularized SEL, adds, "Most of us have assumed that the kind of academic learning that goes on in school has little or nothing to do with one's emotions or social environment. Now, neuroscience is telling us exactly the opposite. The emotional centers of the brain are intricately interwoven with the neocortical areas involved in cognitive learning." As adults, we may find it difficult to focus on work after a bad day or a traumatic event. Similarly, student learning is impacted by their emotions. By teaching students how to deal with their emotions in a healthy way, they will reap the benefits academically as well.

SEL is doing the work to make sure students can be successful at home, with their friends, at school, in sports, in relationships, and in life. The skills are typically separated into five competencies: self-awareness, self-management, social awareness, relationship skills, and responsible decision-making.

Introduction (cont.)

Social-Emotional Competencies

SELF-MANAGEMENT
Manage your emotions, thoughts, and behaviors. Set and work toward goals.

SOCIAL AWARENESS
Take on the perspectives of others, especially those who are different from you. Understand societal expectations and know where to get support.

SELF-AWARENESS
Recognize your own emotions, thoughts, and values. Assess your strengths and weaknesses. Have a growth mindset.

RESPONSIBLE DECISION-MAKING
Make positive choices based on established norms. Understand and consider consequences.

RELATIONSHIP SKILLS
Establish and maintain relationships with others. Communicate effectively and negotiate conflict as necessary.

SEL COMPETENCIES

Each SEL competency helps support child development in life-long learning. SEL helps students develop the skills to have rich connections with their emotional lives and build robust emotional vocabularies. These competencies lead to some impressive data to support students being successful in school and in life.

- Students who learn SEL skills score an average of 11 percentage points higher on standardized tests.

- They are less likely to get office referrals and will spend more time in class.

- These students are more likely to want to come to school and report being happier while at school.

- Educators who teach SEL skills report a 77 percent increase in job satisfaction. (Durlack, et al. 2011)

Your SEL Skills

Educators, parents, and caretakers have a huge part to play as students develop SEL skills. Parker Palmer (2007) reminds us that what children do is often a reflection of what they see and experience. When you stay calm, name your feelings, practice clear communication, and problem-solve in a way that students see, then they reflect that modeling in their own relationships. As you guide students in how to handle conflicts, you can keep a growth mindset and know that with practice, your students can master any skill.

Scenarios

There are many benefits to teaching SEL, from how students behave at home to how they will succeed in life. Let's think about how children with strong SEL skills would react to common life experiences.

At Home

Kyle wakes up. He uses self-talk and says to himself, *I am going to do my best today.* He gets out of bed, picks out his own clothes to wear, and gets ready. As he sits down for breakfast, his little sister knocks over his glass of milk. He thinks, *Uggh, she is so messy! But that's ok—it was just an accident.* Then, he tells his parent and helps clean up the mess.

When his parent picks Kyle up from school, Kyle asks how they are feeling and answers questions about how his day has gone. He says that he found the reading lesson hard, but he used deep breathing and asked questions to figure out new words today.

As his family is getting dinner ready, he sees that his parent is making something he really doesn't like. He stomps his foot in protest, and then he goes to sit in his room for a while. When he comes out, he asks if they can make something tomorrow that he likes.

When he is getting ready for bed, he is silly and playful. He wants to read and point out how each person in the book is feeling. His parent asks him how he would handle the problem the character is facing, and then they talk about the situation.

At School

Cynthia gets to school a little late, and she has to check into the office. Cynthia is embarrassed about being late but feels safe at school and knows that the people there will welcome her with kindness. She steps into her room, and her class pauses to welcome her. Her teacher says, "I'm so glad you are here today."

Cynthia settles into her morning work. After a few minutes, she comes to a problem she doesn't know how to solve. After she gives it her best try, she asks her teacher for some help. Her teacher supports her learning, and Cynthia feels proud of herself for trying.

As lunchtime nears, Cynthia realizes she forgot her lunch in the car. She asks her teacher to call her mom. Her mom says she can't get away and that Cynthia is going to have to eat the school lunch today. Cynthia is frustrated but decides that she is not going to let it ruin her day.

As she is getting ready for school to end, her teacher invites the class to reflect about their day. What is something they are proud of? What is something they wished they could do again? Cynthia thinks about her answers and shares with the class.

These are both pretty dreamy children. The reality is that the development of SEL skills happens in different ways. Some days, students will shock you by how they handle a problem. Other times, they will dig in and not use the skills you teach them. One of the benefits of teaching SEL is that when a student is melting down, your mindset shifts to *I wonder how I can help them learn how to deal with this* rather than *I'm going to punish them so they don't do this again.* Viewing discipline as an opportunity to teach rather than punish is critical for students to learn SEL.

How to Use This Book

Using the Practice Pages

This series is designed to support the instruction of SEL. It is not a curriculum. The activities will help students practice, learn, and grow their SEL skills. Each week is set up for students to practice all five SEL competencies.

 Day 1—Self-Awareness

 Day 2—Self-Management

 Day 3—Social Awareness

 Day 4—Relationship Skills

 Day 5—Responsible Decision-Making

Each of the five competencies has subcategories that are used to target specific skills each day. See the chart on pages 10–11 for a list of which skills are used throughout the book.

Each week also has a theme. These themes rotate and are repeated several times throughout the book. The following themes are included in this book:

- self
- family
- friends
- school
- community
- state
- country
- world

This book also features one week that focuses on online safety.

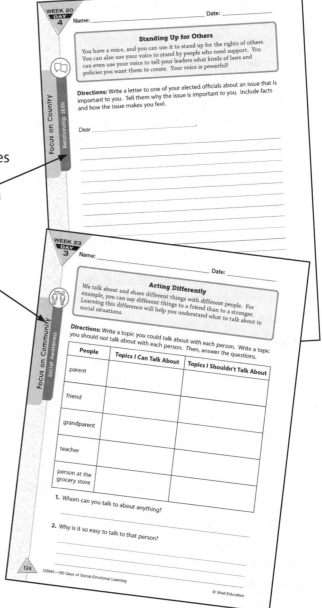

How to Use This Book *(cont.)*

Using the Resources

Rubrics for connecting to self, relating to others, and making decisions can be found on pages 200–202 and in the Digital Resources. Use the rubrics to consider student work. Be sure to share these rubrics with students so that they know what is expected of them.

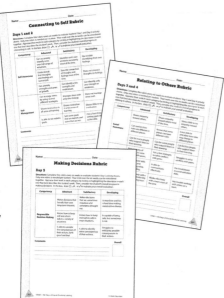

Diagnostic Assessment

Educators can use the pages in this book as diagnostic assessments. The data analysis tools included with this book enable teachers or parents/caregivers to quickly assess students' work and monitor their progress. Educators can quickly see which skills students may need to target further to develop proficiency.

Students will learn how to connect with their own emotions, how to connect with the emotions of others, and how to make good decisions. Assess student learning in each area using the rubrics on pages 200–202. Then, record their overall progress on the analysis sheets on pages 203–205. These charts are also provided in the Digital Resources as PDFs and Microsoft Excel® files.

To Complete the Analyses:

- Write or type students' names in the far-left column. Depending on the number of students, more than one copy of each form may be needed.

- The weeks in which students should be assessed are indicated in the first rows of the charts. Students should be assessed at the ends of those weeks.

- Review students' work for the day(s) indicated in the corresponding rubric. For example, if using the Making Decisions Analysis sheet for the first time, review students' work from Day 5 for all six weeks.

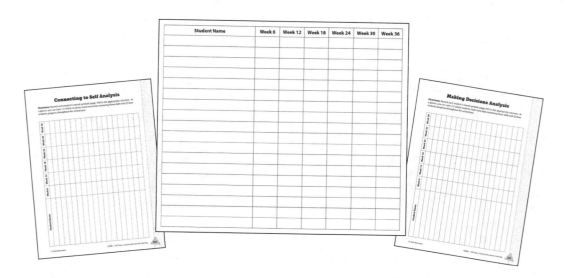

Integrating SEL into Your Teaching

Student self-assessment is key for SEL skills. If students can make accurate evaluations of how they are feeling, then they can work to manage their emotions. If they can manage their emotions, they are more likely to have better relationship skills and make responsible decisions. Children can self-assess from a very young age. The earlier you get them into this practice, the more they will use it and benefit from it for the rest of their lives. The following are some ways you can quickly and easily integrate student self-assessment into your daily routines.

Feelings Check-Ins

Using a scale can be helpful for a quick check-in. After an activity, ask students to rate how they are feeling. Focusing students' attention on how they are feeling helps support their self-awareness. Discuss how students' feelings change as they do different things. Provide students with a visual scale to support these check-ins. These could be taped to their desks or posted in your classroom. Full-color versions of the following scales can be found in the Digital Resources.

- **Emoji:** Having students point to different emoji faces is an easy way to use a rating scale with young students.

- **Symbols:** Symbols, such as weather icons, can also represent students' emotions.

- **Color Wheel:** A color wheel, where different colors represent different emotions, is another effective scale.

- **Numbers:** Have students show 1–5 fingers, with 5 being *I'm feeling great* to 1 being *I'm feeling awful*.

Integrating SEL into Your Teaching *(cont.)*

Reflection

Reflecting is the process of looking closely or deeply at something. When you prompt students with reflection questions, you are supporting this work. Here is a list of questions to get the reflection process started:

- What did you learn from this work?
- What are you proud of in this piece?
- What would you have done differently?
- What was the most challenging part?
- How could you improve this work?
- How did other people help you finish this work?
- How will doing your best on this assignment help you in the future?

Pan Balance

Have students hold out their arms on both sides of their bodies. Ask them a reflection question that has two possible answers. Students should respond by tipping one arm lower than the other (as if one side of the scale is heavier). Here are some example questions:

- Did you talk too much or too little?
- Were you distracted or engaged?
- Did you rush or take too much time?
- Did you stay calm or get angry?
- Was your response safe or unsafe?

Calibrating Student Assessments

Supporting student self-assessment means calibrating their thinking. You will have students who make mistakes but evaluate themselves as though they have never made a mistake in their lives. At the other end of the spectrum, you will likely see students who will be too hard on themselves. In both these cases, having a periodic calibration can help to support accuracy in their evaluations. The *Calibrating Student Assessments* chart is provided in the Digital Resources (calibrating.pdf).

Teaching Assessment

In addition to assessing students, consider the effectiveness of your own instruction. The *Teaching Rubric* can be found in the Digital Resources (teachingrubric.pdf). Use this tool to evaluate your SEL instruction. You may wish to complete this rubric at different points throughout the year to track your progress.

Skills Alignment

Each activity in this book is aligned to a CASEL competency. Within each competency, students will learn a variety of skills. Here are some of the important skills students will practice during the year.

 Self-Awareness

Identifying Emotions	Identifying Bias
Personal and Social Identities	Identifying Prejudice and Discrimination
Honesty	Identifying Strengths
Integrity	Role Models
Growth Mindset	Interests
Understanding One's Emotions	

 Self-Management

Managing Emotions	Controlling Feelings
Planning and Organizing	Self-Talk
Taking Initiative	Calming Down
Managing Stress	Identifying Triggers
Setting and Managing Goals	Trying New Things
Self-Discipline	Collective Agency

 Social Awareness

Taking Others' Perspectives	Advocating for Oneself
Recognizing Others' Strengths	Understanding Different Rules
Empathy	Taking Chances
Gratitude	Systems
Understanding Others' Feelings	

Skills Alignment *(cont.)*

 Relationship Skills

Communication	Teamwork
Positive Relationships	Overcoming Peer Pressure
Standing Up for Others	Helping Others
Seeking and Offering Help	Making Friends
Leadership	Collaboration

 Responsible Decision-Making

Solving Problems	Thoughtfulness
Identifying Solutions	Prioritizing
Being Open-Minded	Considering One's Actions
Using Facts	Identifying Problems
Anticipating Consequences	

Name: _____ **Date:** _____

Identifying Your Emotions

We are all born with the ability to feel five base emotions. They are joy, anger, fear, disgust, and sadness. All the emotions you feel are connected to these base feelings. Naming your emotions can help you understand what you are feeling.

Directions: Read the list of emotions. Write them in the correct columns.

Joy 😄	Anger 😠	Fear 😨	Disgust 🤢	Sadness 😣

cheerful	frightful	panicked
concerned	fuming	raging
content	furious	repulsed
delighted	happy	sickened
depressed	horrified	terrified
devastated	mad	thrilled
exasperated	miserable	upset

Name: _____ Date: _____

Controlling Your Emotions

It is normal to feel a lot of emotions throughout the day. You can help manage all those emotions if you understand how your body feels for each one. Think about a time when you were really upset. How did your body react? Some people feel anger all over their bodies. When you think about how your body reacts to anger, where do you notice it most?

Directions: Think about a time when you felt each of these feelings strongly. Write the body part where you felt the emotion. Then, describe what you felt. Follow the example.

Example:

Emotion: nervous

Body Part: _stomach_

What I Felt: _tight and achy_

1. **Emotion:** anger

   Body Part: _____

   What I Felt: _____

2. **Emotion:** fear

   Body Part: _____

   What I Felt: _____

3. **Emotion:** excitement

   Body Part: _____

   What I Felt: _____

Focus on Self
Self-Management

Name: _____ Date: _____

Taking Others' Perspectives

People may respond to the same situation in different ways. It is important to understand how others feel. This will help you understand their *perspectives*, or points of view. Noticing body language is one way to see how others feel.

Directions: Describe how the people in each picture are feeling.

1.

_____

_____

3.

_____

_____

2.

_____

_____

4.

_____

_____

Communicating Effectively

People communicate in all sorts of ways. Sometimes, they talk for hours. Sometimes, they do not use any words at all. This is called *nonverbal communication*. It is helpful to know how people communicate without words. It will help you communicate better.

Directions: Answer the questions to show how your body would communicate with these friends.

You arrive at school really tired and sad. You just had an argument with someone at home. Your friend is excited to talk about their favorite TV show.

1. What would your body be doing?

_____

2. How would your body show how you feel?

_____

_____

A friend borrowed your art supplies without asking. You are feeling angry. When you confront them about the supplies, you also learn that many of them are broken.

3. What would your body be doing?

_____

4. How would your body show how you feel?

_____

_____

Name: _____   Date: _____

Solving Problems

Some problems are small issues that you can solve on your own. Some problems are big issues that require help. You need to determine if each problem is a small or big issue. This will help you decide how to solve it.

Focus on Self

Responsible Decision-Making

Directions: Circle whether each problem is small or big.

1. You are working on a computer at school when your program freezes and tells you to restart.

   small problem   big problem

2. You miss your bus and are stuck at the school after soccer practice. You do not have a phone, and the building is locked.

   small problem   big problem

3. You have an argument with a friend. They say something hurtful to you.

   small problem   big problem

4. You see someone taking things from other people's backpacks.

   small problem   big problem

Directions: Choose one of the small problems, and write the steps you would take to solve it.

_____

_____

_____

_____

Name: _____ **Date:** _____

Identifying Emotions

We feel most of our big emotions when we are at home. We feel safe there to let everything out. When you can identify what you are feeling, you can be a better family member.

Directions: Describe how you would feel if each situation happened to you.

1. You come home on your birthday, open the door, and SURPRISE! Your family has thrown you a surprise party.

   _____

   _____

2. You are going to a weeklong summer camp away from your family. None of your friends will be there.

   _____

   _____

3. You are looking forward to going to your grandmother's home. You start to feel sick and have to stay home.

   _____

   _____

Directions: Draw yourself in one of these situations. Make sure to show your feelings in your picture.

Focus on Family

Self-Awareness

Name: _____ Date: _____

Controlling Your Feelings

You get to choose how to respond to your strong feelings. You can let your feelings get bigger and bigger inside you. Or you can work to manage your emotions. One way to do that is called *self-talk*. This is when you tell yourself calming messages. These positive thoughts help you feel better. They can also help you be more in control of your emotions.

Directions: Read each situation. Write two self-talk messages that each person could tell themself to calm down.

1. Dana's best friend said her parents are getting her a cell phone. When Dana gets home from school, she asks her parents if they would get her a cell phone. Dana's parents tell her that she is too young for a phone. She feels very angry and thinks their decision is unfair.

   _____

   _____

   _____

   _____

   _____

2. Miles is really excited about a trip to visit his cousins in another state. Two days before Miles leaves, his parents tell him that the trip has been canceled. His cousins are all sick. Miles feels very sad and disappointed.

   _____

   _____

   _____

   _____

   _____

Name: _____ **Date:** _____

The Feelings of Others

Family members will have different feelings. Even in the same moment, they may see things in different ways. Stop and think about how your family members see things. This will help you understand them. It will also lead to stronger relationships.

Directions: Underline clues in the story that show how the people are feeling. Then, answer the questions.

Chore Battle

Sara and Joey are doing their chores at home. Sara is sweeping the floor, and Joey is cleaning the dishes. Joey is standing at the sink washing dishes when Sara asks him to move so she can sweep. Joey doesn't want to stop washing dishes to move. He wants to finish the dishes as fast as possible so he can go hang out with his friends. He rolls his eyes at Sara and moves just a little bit. Sara also wants to finish her chores so she can go read her book, so she bangs Joey's leg with the broom. Joey shouts at Sara to stop hitting him. Sara mutters under her breath that he should get out of her way.

1. How is Sara feeling?

_____

2. How do you know?

_____

_____

3. How is Joey feeling?

_____

4. How do you know?

_____

_____

Name: _____ Date: _____

Communication Skills

Communication is when one person sends a message to another. The person who sends the message is the sender. The person who gets it is the receiver.

Directions: Read each situation. Write who is the sender, who is the receiver, and what the message is. Then, write your own example.

1. Elena and Luis are talking. Elena is describing the plot of the book she is reading.

   Sender: _____

   Receiver: _____

   Message: _____

2. Shawn is angry that his parents won't let him hang out with his friends. He yells at his mom that it is unfair to make him stay home.

   Sender: _____

   Receiver: _____

   Message: _____

3. Monique is on the phone with her grandma. Her grandma tells her about the vegetables she planted in her garden.

   Sender: _____

   Receiver: _____

   Message: _____

4. _____

   _____

   Sender: _____

   Receiver: _____

   Message: _____

Identifying Solutions

A conflict happens when two or more people do not agree. Conflict can be uncomfortable. But it can also be a chance to learn about yourself and others.

Directions: In the smaller circles, write six words that come to mind when you think of the word *conflict*. Then, follow the steps.

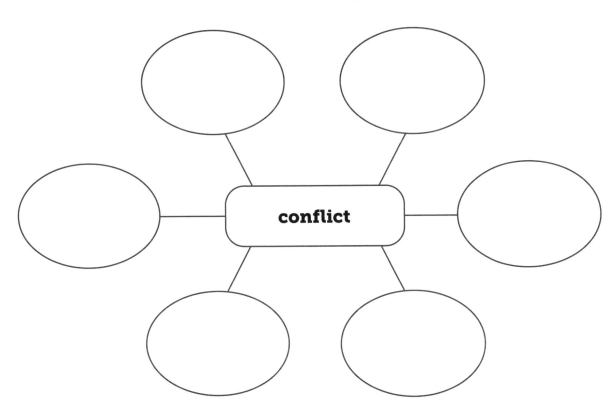

Focus on Family
Responsible Decision-Making

1. Write a star next to any words that are positive.

2. Describe something good that can happen because of a conflict. For example, you and a friend might have a stronger friendship after solving a conflict.

_____

_____

_____

_____

Name: _____ Date: _____

Focus on Community

Self-Awareness

The Benefits of Culture

Your culture includes all the ways your way of life is unique. People in the same community may have different cultures. Culture includes the holidays you celebrate and how you celebrate them. It includes the food you eat and how you dress. It affects what you do every day. Culture can be an asset. An *asset* is something valuable or beneficial.

Directions: Write your culture's traditions next to each event. Write another important part of your culture on the last line.

1. Birthdays: _____

_____

2. Special Meals: _____

_____

3. How You Dress: _____

_____

4. Important Holidays: _____

_____

5. _____

_____

Directions: Work with a partner. List one way your cultures or traditions are the same. List one way they are different.

6. Same: _____

_____

_____

7. Different: _____

_____

_____

Name: _____ Date: _____

Planning and Organizational Skills

Being able to organize your schedule is an important life skill. This will help you know what you are doing each day. This will also help you be on time and will ensure you don't miss anything.

Directions: Choose three events to put on your calendar. Write the name and time of each activity on the right day. Be careful not to schedule yourself to be in more than one place at a time.

Monday	Tuesday	Wednesday	Thursday	Friday

Community Activities

1. Jesse's birthday party, Friday, 4:00–6:00 p.m.
2. reading group at the library, Tuesday, 2:00–3:00 p.m.
3. soccer at the park, Thursday, 11:00 a.m.–12:00 p.m.
4. volunteer at homeless shelter, Tuesday, 1:30–3:30 p.m.
5. music concert, Friday, 5:00–6:00 p.m.
6. José's piano recital, Monday, 3:00–5:00 p.m.
7. basketball at the community center, Thursday, 11:30 a.m.–12:30 p.m.
8. biking, Monday, 2:00–4:00 p.m.

Focus on Community

Self-Management

Name: _____ **Date:** _____

Recognizing Strengths in Others

You have many strengths. So do the other people in your community. They use their strengths to make your community a better place.

Focus on Community

Social Awareness

Directions: Write which place in your community should get each award and why. Then, make up your own award.

1. Best Restaurant: _____

Why? _____

_____

2. Best Park: _____

Why? _____

_____

3. Best Grocery Store: _____

Why? _____

_____

4. Best Place to Hang Out: _____

Why? _____

_____

5. Best _____ : _____

Why? _____

_____

Name: _____ **Date:** _____

Developing Positive Relationships

Getting to know people in your community is one way you can make your community better. It can also make you feel good. Meeting new people can be difficult. But if you take the first step, you may find that you will connect with others and make new friends.

Directions: Write what each person could do to make a connection in their community.

1. Allison is trying out for the volleyball team. She does not know anyone who plays volleyball. When she arrives at the gym, she sees people warming up together. What could Allison do to make a connection?

   _____

   _____

   _____

2. Max is visiting his dad. He decides to play outside while his dad takes a phone call. Max sees a group of kids playing on their bikes. He really wants to play with the kids, but he is nervous. What could Max do to make a connection?

   _____

   _____

   _____

3. Fatima just started a new school. She gets to the lunchroom and freezes. She doesn't have anyone to sit with. She sees an open seat next to a kid from her science class. What could Fatima do to make a connection?

   _____

   _____

   _____

Name: _____ Date: _____

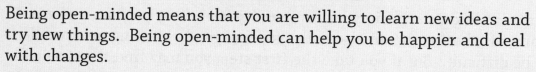

Trying New Things

Being open-minded means that you are willing to learn new ideas and try new things. Being open-minded can help you be happier and deal with changes.

Directions: Write a short story about something new you would like to try in your community. Draw the new thing you would like to try.

_____

_____

_____

_____

_____

_____

_____

_____

_____

_____

_____

126961—180 Days of Social-Emotional Learning

© Shell Education

Name: _____ Date: _____

Benefits of Being Bilingual

Some people speak more than one language. Speaking two languages is called being bilingual. This skill is an asset. An asset is a strength, something valuable, or something that benefits you. Being bilingual means that you can communicate with more people. Many people in your state are bilingual.

Directions: Read each scenario, and answer the questions.

1. Maria stops at the grocery store owned by the Kim family. She wants to try something new for dinner. She can't read the labels on the food in the store. They are written in another language.

   Why would it be helpful for Maria to know another language?

   _____

   _____

   _____

2. Andrew is walking along the street when he sees two people looking at a map. They are obviously lost. But they do not speak the same language as Andrew.

   Why would it be helpful for Andrew to know another language?

   _____

   _____

   _____

3. What other language would you like to learn? How would it be an asset to you?

   _____

   _____

   _____

Focus on State

Self-Awareness

Name: _____ Date: _____

Planning and Organization

Being organized is good for you. It helps you spend more time on important things. It also helps you communicate clearly.

Directions: Imagine a friend is visiting from another state. Write five things you would take them to see and do. Start with the most important. Finish with the least important. Then, draw your favorite idea.

Things to Do in My State

1. _____

2. _____

3. _____

4. _____

5. _____

Focus on State

Self-Management

Name: _____ Date: _____

Recognizing Strengths in Others

There are many people who help make your state a safe place to live. The governor leads the state. State troopers keep the state and highways safe, and judges determine when someone has broken a law. Social workers make sure people are safe where they live. Park rangers keep parks clean and safe. Engineers help design bridges, dams, and other things people use every day. All these people have strengths that make them good at their jobs.

Focus on State

Social Awareness

Directions: Write a character trait from the list that would be a good strength for a person in each job.

compassionate	leader
courageous	quick thinking
fair	reliable
good communicator	respectful
honest	strong
intelligent	thoughtful

Jobs

1. Governor: _____

2. Social Worker: _____

3. Judge: _____

4. Park Ranger: _____

5. State Trooper: _____

6. Engineer: _____

7. Construction Worker: _____

Name: _____ Date: _____

Developing Positive Relationships

One way to develop relationships is to spend time with others. You can do this in many ways. For example, you can volunteer or visit a relative.

Directions: Answer the questions to make a plan to get to know someone in your community. Share your plan with a partner. Then, make changes to improve your plan.

1. Who do you want to get to know better?

_____

2. Write two ways you can make that relationship stronger.

_____

_____

_____

_____

3. How will you implement your plan?

_____

_____

4. When will you implement your plan?

_____

5. After working with your partner, write how you will make your plan better.

_____

_____

_____

Curiosity and Open-Mindedness

Being curious makes life more fun. It is exciting to think about new places to visit. Your state is a great place to start. There are many interesting places that you may never have visited.

Directions: Write two places in your state that you've never been to but would like to visit. Write what you would do there and whom you would take with you. If you do not know where to start, search online.

First Place: _____

Activity: _____
_____

Person: _____

Second Place: _____

Activity: _____
_____

Person: _____

Directions: Draw yourself visiting one of the places you listed.

Focus on State

Responsible Decision-Making

Name: _____ Date: _____

Personal and Social Identities

Your *identity* is the set of qualities and beliefs that make you unique. It is how you see yourself. Identity can come from groups we belong to. It can come from our beliefs and our families. Your identity can include languages you speak, your culture, and your religion. It can also include your hobbies and your personality. Everyone has many identities.

Focus on Country

Self-Awareness

Directions: Draw stars by the identities that describe you.

Identities		
artist	cautious	shy
athlete	friend	sister
boy	girl	stepbrother
brave	intelligent	stepsister
brother	outgoing	student

Directions: Write at least three other identities that describe you. Then, draw a picture showing one of your identities.

_____

_____

_____

Courage to Take Initiative

Taking *initiative* means to take action. Sometimes, this can be a scary thing to do. It is especially scary when you are trying something new.

People have changed history by having courage to stand up for what they believe. Ida B. Wells is known for standing up for women's right to vote. Wells also spoke up against the unfair treatment of Black Americans. She is remembered for her strong voice and her great courage.

Directions: Answer the questions to describe a time when you were brave.

1. What did you do that was brave?

_____

_____

_____

2. How did you feel before you did this?

_____

_____

_____

3. How did you feel afterward?

_____

_____

_____

4. How did this experience help you be brave other times?

_____

_____

_____

Focus on Country

Self-Management

Name: _____ **Date:** _____

Empathy and Compassion

Having empathy means you are able to put yourself in someone else's shoes. You may not have experienced what someone else is feeling. But you can still understand their feelings.

Directions: Imagine a friend's house has been destroyed by a hurricane. Think about how they must be feeling. Write your friend a letter that shows empathy for their situation. Include a picture to go with your letter.

Dear _____ ,

_____

_____

_____

_____

_____

_____

_____

Your friend,

_____

Name: _____ Date: _____

Standing Up for the Rights of Others

Sometimes, we encounter things in life that are not fair. You may even see someone else being treated unfairly. You can stand up for other people and help them.

Claudette Colvin was a high school student in Montgomery, Alabama, in 1955. At that time, Black people had to ride in the back of the bus. Claudette was the first person to challenge that law. She was arrested when she refused to give up her seat. She stood up for herself and for others. Because of her courage, other people protested the same unfair law.

Directions: Write a newspaper article about someone who stands up for other people. Include what they do for others and how they make the world a better place.

Article Title: _____

" ALL THE NEWS
YOU NEED TO KNOW "

News·Today

_____

_____

_____

_____

_____

_____

_____

_____

_____

_____

_____

Name: _____ Date: _____

Focus on Country

Responsible Decision-Making

Using Facts to Make Decisions

Making decisions can be hard. Using data and facts can help you make better decisions. Elected officials make laws that citizens have to follow. They make these laws after much research and looking at data and facts. It can take a long time to create new laws.

Directions: Imagine you are a member of Congress and you want to write a new law that will keep people safe or make people's lives better. Answer the questions about your law.

1. Describe your new law.

_____

_____

_____

2. What information would you need to make the best law possible?

_____

_____

_____

3. How would this law improve people's lives?

_____

_____

_____

Directions: Draw a poster on a separate sheet of paper to help get people excited for your new law.

Name: _____ **Date:** _____

Personal and Social Identities

How you see yourself affects the choices you make. If you see yourself as kind, you are more likely to be kind to others.

Directions: Draw yourself, and write words around your picture that describe you.

Directions: Choose one of the words. Describe a time when you showed that quality to others.

_____

_____

_____

_____

_____

Name: _____ Date: _____

Stress Management Strategies

Stress is a normal part of daily life. Stress can be good when it motivates us. It can help us to think more quickly in new and exciting situations. But bad stress can make us scared or anxious, and it can be bad for our health. Knowing how to manage stress will help your body feel better and your mind feel calmer.

Directions: Follow the prompts to practice deep belly breathing.

1. Check in with your body. In one word, how are you feeling?

   _____

2. Put one hand on your chest and one hand on your belly. Notice where you feel movement when you breathe in. Are you taking deep breaths from your belly? Or shallow breaths from your chest?

   _____

3. Focus on taking a big, deep breath from the bottom of your belly. Breathe so deeply that your hand on your belly moves.

   _____

4. Take a few more deep breaths from your belly, and close your eyes. Check in with your body again. In one word, how are you feeling now?

   _____

5. How did your feelings change?

   _____

   _____

6. How could you use belly breathing when you feel stressed?

   _____

   _____

Name: _____ **Date:** _____

Showing Gratitude

Gratitude means to be thankful for something or someone. You can show your gratitude many ways. You can say thank you, or you can make something. You can also write a thank you note.

Directions: Write a letter to someone you would like to thank. Be specific about why you are thanking them. Write about what they did to make you feel gratitude.

Dear _____ ,

_____

_____

_____

_____

_____

_____

_____

_____

_____

_____

Sincerely,

_____

Focus on Self

Social Awareness

Name: _____   Date: _____

Focus on Self

Relationship Skills

Effective Communication Skills

Listening is an important part of communication. You are more likely to understand a message if you listen closely. But if you are thinking about what to say next, you are not really listening. It takes a lot of work and a lot of focus to be a good listener.

Directions: Work with a partner to practice listening. One person will be the talker, and the other will be the listener. Have the talker speak for a few minutes about their favorite thing to do. The listener should not say anything, but they should show that they are listening. Switch roles, and do the activity again. Then, answer the questions.

1. When you were the talker, how did it feel to have someone listen to you so closely?

   _____

   _____

2. How did it feel to be the listener? Was it hard to stay quiet?

   _____

   _____

3. How does having good listening skills help you communicate with someone else?

   _____

   _____

4. Draw a picture to show what good listening looks like.

   ┌───┐
   │   │
   │   │
   │   │
   │   │
   │   │
   └───┘

Name: _____ Date: _____

Identifying Solutions

The way people react to a problem determines whether the problem is solved. An overreaction is when someone reacts too strongly to a situation. This makes the problem bigger. An appropriate reaction is when the reaction matches the size of the problem. This helps solve problems.

Directions: Write an overreaction for each conflict. Then, write an appropriate reaction. Follow the example.

Example:

You forgot to bring your homework on the day it is due.

Overreaction: _I am never going to pass this class!_

Appropriate Reaction: _It's just one assignment. Maybe my teacher will let_

me turn it in tomorrow.

---

1. You hear someone say your name. But you can't hear what else they are saying.

   Overreaction: _____

   Appropriate Reaction: _____

2. Your friend chooses to sit with someone else at lunch.

   Overreaction: _____

   Appropriate Reaction: _____

3. You see your sibling playing with your game after you asked them not to touch it.

   Overreaction: _____

   Appropriate Reaction: _____

4. Your coach tells you to sit on the sidelines for a few minutes during a game.

   Overreaction: _____

   Appropriate Reaction: _____

Responsible Decision-Making

Focus on Self

Name: _____ Date: _____

Personal and Social Identities

How others see you affects how they act toward you. You can impact how people see you by being aware of how you act around them.

Directions: How would your friends describe you? Brainstorm a list of words that you think they would use. Then, draw yourself as your friends see you.

_____

_____

_____

_____

Focus on Friends

Self-Awareness

Name: _____ Date: _____

Personal and Collective Goals

Working together on a goal can help accomplish the goal more quickly. It can also be a lot of fun. To achieve a goal as a group, you need to be organized and plan your steps so that everyone can help.

Directions: Write the steps you and your friends need to take to see a concert. Include who will help you with each step.

Goal: Go to a Concert

Step 1: Get Permission

1. How will you ask for permission? What will you say to convince your caregivers to let you go? _____

_____

2. How can your friends help with this step? _____

_____

Step 2: Pay for Tickets

3. How will you pay for the tickets? What can you do to get the money?

_____

_____

4. How can your friends help with this step? _____

Step 3: Get to the Concert

5. How will you and your friends get to the concert? _____

_____

6. How can your friends help with this step? _____

_____

. . . .

Challenge: What might be missing from your plan? What problems may occur? How can you prepare for them? Answer these questions on a separate sheet of paper.

Focus on Friends
Self-Management

Name: _____ Date: _____

Focus on Friends · Social Awareness

Empathy

Having empathy means that you can understand how others feel. You can do this even if you haven't experienced the same things as someone else.

Directions: Write dialogue for each situation. Add your friend's dialogue first. Then, add what you would say to show your concern for your friend's feelings. Be empathetic.

1. Your friend just failed a big test. They are really worried that their parents are going to be upset.

2. Your friend tells you that someone is making fun of them. They are very upset about it.

Directions: Choose one of the two situations. Describe how you think your friend would feel after you showed empathy.

_____

_____

Name: _____ **Date:** _____

Effective Communication

There are things you can do to communicate better. There are also things you can do to make it worse. This will either make it easier or harder for a receiver to understand your message.

Directions: Write each action in the correct column.

Good Communication	Poor Communication

asking questions when a person is done talking

making eye contact

assuming you know what a person will say

looking down at the floor

speaking clearly

crossing your arms

Directions: Answer the questions.

1. How do you feel when someone uses good communication with you?

_____

_____

2. How do you feel when someone uses poor communication with you?

_____

_____

Name: _____ Date: _____

Focus on Friends

Responsible Decision-Making

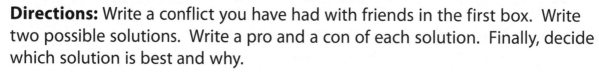

Identifying Solutions

There are many ways to solve a problem. A valuable problem-solving skill is being able to decide which solution is best.

Directions: Write a conflict you have had with friends in the first box. Write two possible solutions. Write a pro and a con of each solution. Finally, decide which solution is best and why.

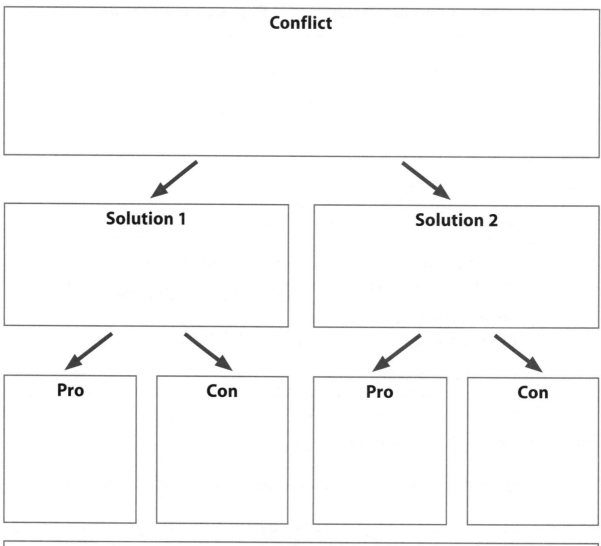

Conflict

Solution 1

Solution 2

Pro

Con

Pro

Con

Best Solution and Why

Name: _____ Date: _____

Honesty and Integrity

A person with integrity is someone who is honest. They will always try to do what is right.

Directions: Read the text, and answer the questions.

The Broken Window

Jake and Juan are playing baseball in their street. Jake hits a line drive straight into a parked car. The ball shatters the window. The boys know the car belongs to their neighbor, Mr. Salvador. They are afraid to tell Mr. Salvador what happened.

1. What is the problem?

_____

_____

2. How would the boys respond if they acted out of fear?

_____

_____

_____

3. How would the boys respond if they acted with integrity?

_____

_____

_____

4. How would you respond? Why?

_____

_____

_____

Name: _____ Date: _____

Take Initiative

To take initiative means to take action. Sometimes, it can be scary to take action. It can mean stepping out of your comfort zone. It takes courage to do something new. Some communities have groups that advocate for the people who live there. To advocate is to fight for something. People meet and make decisions to try to make their communities better.

Directions: Answer the questions to show how your community could be better.

1. What could be improved in your community?

   _____

   _____

2. What steps could be taken to make the improvement?

   _____

   _____

3. What could you do to help? How could you advocate?

   _____

   _____

4. Find the name and address of a group in your community that can help you.

   _____

   _____

- -

Challenge: Use your answers to write a letter to your mayor or other leader. Write about the improvements you would like to see. Include how you and other people can help.

Name: _____ **Date:** _____

Different Rules and Expectations

Rules and expectations can vary based on where you are. Your family may have different rules than your school. Your school may have different rules than your community. It is important to know how rules are different so you know what to expect.

Directions: Answer each question about home and school. Then, put your answers in the Venn diagram.

1. What do you eat for lunch at home? _____

2. What do you eat for lunch at school? _____

3. Where do you do your homework? _____

4. Where do you do your schoolwork? _____

5. What is your favorite thing to do at home? _____

6. What is your favorite thing to do at school? _____

7. What is one thing you enjoy doing at home? _____

8. What is one thing you enjoy doing at school? _____

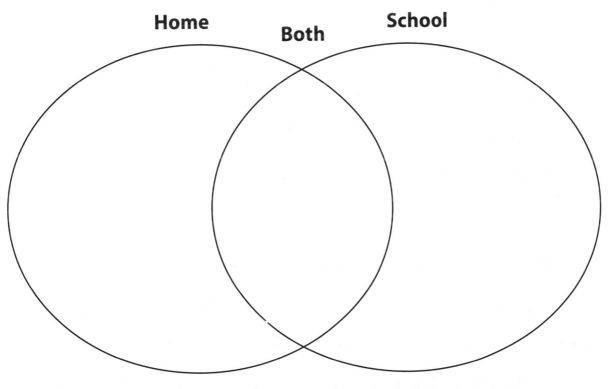

Home   **Both**   **School**

Focus on Community
Social Awareness

Name: _____ Date: _____

Developing Positive Relationships

Strong relationships will support you. They can help you work through challenges. But it takes work to keep those relationships strong.

Directions: Write some of the relationships you have in each category. Leave the Self section blank. Then, answer the questions.

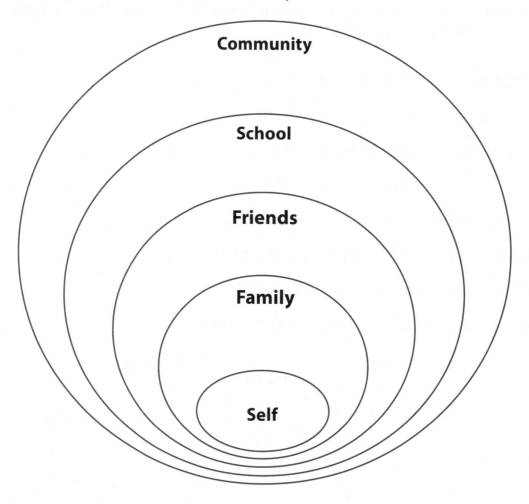

1. Which area has the fewest relationships?

_____

2. How could you improve one of the relationships you listed?

_____

_____

Name: _____ Date: _____

How You Act and Think

Your community can make your life better. One thing your community can do is to offer services to support you and your neighbors. These services can help keep you safe and make life more fun.

Directions: Write how each service makes your community better. Then, answer the question.

_____

_____

_____

_____

_____

_____

_____

_____

1. What do you do to keep your community safe?

_____

_____

Name: _____ **Date:** _____

Cultural and Personal Skills

No matter your age, you can contribute to your state. You have skills and strengths, and you can use them to help others.

The Alaska state flag was created by a 13-year-old boy named Benny Benson. He won a contest in 1927. His design has been used ever since. Think about your skills. Think about how you could make your state better.

Directions: Design a new flag for your state. Show the things that make your state a nice place to live.

Name: _____ Date: _____

Planning and Organizing

Big research projects take a lot of planning and organizing. You need to look up information. You need to decide what is important and what is not. You need to make lists to ensure you don't miss anything.

Directions: Research the facts about your state. Write each fact and where you found it. Use the resources in the box, or use your own.

Resources

audio files	newspaper
encyclopedia	reference book
internet search	textbook

1. **Date of Statehood:** _____

   _____

2. **State Capital:** _____

   _____

3. **State Song:** _____

   _____

4. **State Flower:** _____

   _____

5. **State Bird** _____

   _____

6. **State Flag:** _____

   _____

7. **State Motto:** _____

   _____

Name: _____ Date: _____

How You Act and Feel

Laws can affect how people feel and behave. Many laws are created to help us be safe. Your state creates laws that help you make safe and responsible choices.

Directions: Study each picture. Write how someone could follow a law.

1.

_____

_____

3.

_____

_____

2.

_____

_____

4.

_____

_____

Directions: Answer the questions.

5. How do laws change how people act?

_____

_____

6. Write a law that makes you feel safe.

_____

Name: _____ **Date:** _____

Seeking and Offering Help

Sometimes, people need help from others. Asking for help can be hard, but it is often a good idea. When someone asks you for help, it can make you feel good. It can make you feel needed and useful.

Directions: On the top hand, write five things that you have done to help others. On the bottom hand, write five things that others have done to help you. Think about your family, friends, and community.

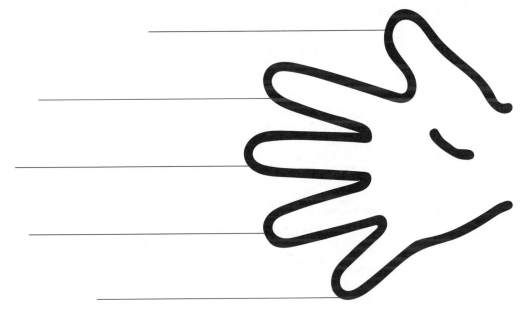

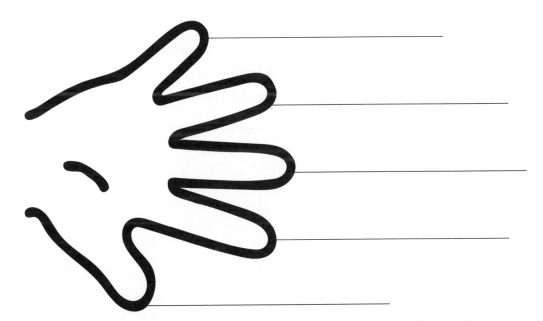

Focus on State
Relationship Skills

Name: _____ **Date:** _____

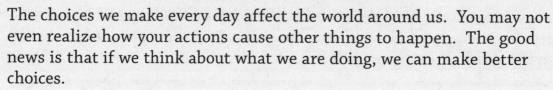

Anticipating Consequences

The choices we make every day affect the world around us. You may not even realize how your actions cause other things to happen. The good news is that if we think about what we are doing, we can make better choices.

Focus on State

Responsible Decision-Making

Directions: Fill in the blanks with phrases from the Word Bank to show the consequences. Follow the example.

Word Bank		
drought	low lakes	using lots of water

Example: ___Using lots of water___ leads to ____low lakes____ which leads to ___drought_____.

Word Bank		
air pollution	a big campfire	smoke in the sky

1. _____ leads to _____ which

   leads to _____.

Word Bank		
eating healthy food	a healthier body	more energy

2. _____ leads to _____ which

   leads to _____.

Name: _____ Date: _____

The Benefits of Where You Live

We all grow up in different places. Every place has something that makes life enjoyable for the people who live there.

There are over 400 sites in the National Park Service. Some are sprawling natural lands. Some are historical sites. They are all places that are so amazing that the government has made them into protected parks for everyone to enjoy.

Directions: Answer the questions about where you live.

1. What is the closest national park to where you live?

   _____

2. How might that park make life better for the people who visit or live near it?

   _____

3. What is another good thing about where you live?

   _____

4. How does that thing make your life better?

   _____

5. Draw where you live. Include things that you like about where you live.

Focus on Country

Self-Awareness

Name: _____ Date: _____

Practicing Self-Discipline

Achieving a goal can take a lot of time and focus. Sometimes, you have to try a few times before you are successful. But if you stick with it, you could achieve your dreams!

Every four years, athletes from around the world compete at the top of their game. Their goal is to represent their countries in the Olympic Games. Athletes train for years to get to the Games. They work through injuries and setbacks while keeping focused on their goals.

Directions: Answer the questions to make a plan to achieve one of your goals.

1. What is your goal?

    _____

2. Describe your plan to achieve your goal.

    _____

    _____

    _____

3. What challenges might come up?

    _____

    _____

4. How will you work through these challenges?

    _____

    _____

    _____

5. Who can help you achieve this goal?

    _____

Name: _____ Date: _____

Unfair Rules

Sometimes, you will experience things that are not fair. When you notice something unfair, you have the power to stand up and try to make it right.

Before 1972, there were often more chances for boys to play sports in school than for girls. That changed with the federal law called *Title 9*. Now, schools must give the same opportunities to boys and girls.

Focus on Country
Social Awareness

Directions: Circle the pictures that are unfair.

Directions: Write something you could do to make the unfair situations fair for everyone.

1. _____

_____

2. _____

_____

Name: _____ Date: _____

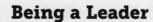

Focus on Country

Relationship Skills

Being a Leader

Leaders show other people the way forward. They may show the way to solve a problem or the way to complete a task. Leaders make sure the groups they are leading achieves their goals. There are many kinds of leaders. The president and members of Congress lead the country. Mayors and city council members lead their cities. Teachers lead their classrooms. You might lead your group in a school project.

Directions: Answer these questions.

1. Whom do you see as a leader in your life?

_____

2. What makes that person a good leader?

_____

_____

3. What or whom would you like to lead? Why?

_____

_____

_____

4. Why would you be a good leader?

_____

_____

_____

5. If you were president, what would you want to change? Why?

_____

_____

_____

Name: _____ Date: _____

Being Thoughtful

It can sometimes be hard to slow down and be thoughtful about your actions. Some decisions are more important than others. You need to take your time and think really hard about those big choices.

Voting is a big decision. When people vote, they are making important decisions for the future of their country and communities.

Directions: Read the text, and answer the questions.

The Library Problem

There was a fire at the library. All of the books are ruined, and the building is not safe to enter. The library is used by the people in town to check out books, have story time for kids, and as a space for students to study. Some people want to open a new library across town. Other people want to fix the library that burned. You have to vote to help the town decide.

1. How would you vote? _____

2. Why did you choose to vote that way?

_____

_____

3. What information helped you make your decision?

_____

_____

_____

4. How would you respond if more people vote for the other idea?

_____

_____

_____

Name: _____ Date: _____

Focus on Self

Self-Awareness

Know How You Feel

Anger is a big emotion that we all feel. We can feel a little angry, really furious, or somewhere in between. Being able to tell how angry you are will help you know how to calm yourself down.

Directions: Color each anger thermometer to the level of anger that each situation would make you feel. Then, answer the questions.

Your partner in a group project does not finish their work.

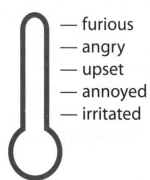

— furious
— angry
— upset
— annoyed
— irritated

Your teacher moves your desk away from your friends.

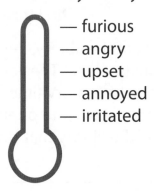

— furious
— angry
— upset
— annoyed
— irritated

Your parent doesn't let you go to a sleepover that all your friends are going to.

— furious
— angry
— upset
— annoyed
— irritated

Someone starts a bad rumor about you at school.

— furious
— angry
— upset
— annoyed
— irritated

1. Which situation would make you the angriest?

_____

_____

2. Why would it make you so angry?

_____

_____

_____

Name: _____ **Date:** _____

Control Your Feelings

We all experience anger, frustration, and other strong emotions. It is helpful to know many ways to calm your body and your mind. This will help you calm down more easily.

Directions: Try these calming exercises. Then, answer the questions.

- **Cool the Cocoa:** This is a deep breathing exercise. Hold your hands in front of you like you are holding a cup of hot cocoa. Take a big deep breath, and blow on your cocoa like you are cooling it down. Do this three times.

- **Muscle Relaxation:** This exercise will help you release tension in your muscles. Start with your face and squeeze all the muscles in your face, and then release. Then, squeeze your shoulders and arms and release. Squeeze your stomach muscles and release. Squeeze your upper legs and release. Squeeze your lower legs and release. Squeeze your feet and release. Finally, squeeze every muscle in your body that you can and release. End with a deep breath.

- **Think Happy Thoughts:** Imagine a place that makes you feel really happy. It could be a beach, the playground, or your grandma's house. Imagine yourself there, and let the happy thoughts fill your mind.

1. How do you feel after these calming exercises?

   _____

   _____

2. When could you use one of these exercises?

   _____

   _____

3. Which exercise would you use?

   _____

Focus on Self

Self-Management

Name: _____ Date: _____

Focus on Self

Social Awareness

The Feelings of Others

Your behavior affects other people. The things you do impact how other people feel and the choices they make.

Directions: Predict how your actions would make someone feel and act in each situation.

You borrow your friend's sweatshirt. While you are wearing it, you stain the front and rip the sleeve.

1. How would your actions make your friend feel?

_____

2. What might your friend do next time you ask to borrow something?

_____

Your friend tells you a secret and asks you to keep it to yourself. You tell their secret to someone else.

3. How would your actions make your friend feel?

_____

4. What might your friend do next time they had a secret?

_____

You stick up for your friend when other people are teasing them at school.

5. How would your actions make your friend feel?

_____

6. How might your friend treat you in the future?

_____

Name: _____ Date: _____

Working as a Team

Members of the same team may have different ideas. That can cause conflict. But good communication helps teams work together well. One good way to communicate is with an I-message. This is when you state how you feel when something happens: "I feel…." Then, you suggest how you would like to do it differently next time. I-messages show how you feel instead of blaming others.

Example: I feel sad when you don't share with me. Next time, will you let me use your markers?

Directions: Read the text. Then, complete the I-messages for Kent and Julia.

Building a Volcano

Kent and Julia are working on a science project. They need to make an erupting volcano. Kent wants to jump right in and start building the volcano, but he needs Julia's help. Julia wants to wait and learn how to make the lava erupt. She needs it quiet to focus on learning the process.

1. **Kent:** I feel _____ when _____.

   Next time, _____.

2. **Julia:** I feel _____ when _____.

   Next time, _____.

3. Suggest how Kent and Julia can solve their problem and work together.

   _____

   _____

   _____

Directions: Write an I-message you could use with someone you know.

4. **Person:** _____

   I feel _____ when _____.

   Next time, _____.

Name: _____ Date: _____

Good Choices

Making good choices means you think about how your actions affect others. Even good choices impact other people.

Directions: Identify each problem. Write a solution. Write an impact it may have.

You have been on the same basketball team for years. You really want to try out for band. But band practice is at the same time.

1. What is the problem? _____

_____

2. What is one possible solution? _____

_____

3. What is the impact of that solution? Whom might this decision affect?

_____

_____

You find a wallet on your walk to school. There is money and an ID in it. Your friend suggests taking the money.

4. What is the problem? _____

_____

5. What is one possible solution? _____

_____

6. What is the impact of that solution? Whom might this decision affect?

_____

_____

Name: _____ Date: _____

Growth Mindset

Having a growth mindset means you are flexible in your thinking. You know that you can grow and change and learn new things. The opposite of a growth mindset is a fixed mindset. When you have a fixed mindset, you believe things will always be a certain way and will never change.

Directions: Draw a line from each thought to the mindset it represents.

I am struggling with math. I know I can get better if I try.

I am never going to make a new friend. I am going to be alone forever.

If I stay calm and focus, I will be able to figure out this problem.

I am feeling really angry right now. When I wake up tomorrow, things will seem better.

This test is so hard. I am going to fail no matter what.

I hate running. I am never going to get faster.

Growth Mindset

Fixed Mindset

Directions: Write two examples of a growth mindset that would help you.

1. _____

_____

2. _____

_____

Name: _____ Date: _____

Focus on School

Self-Management

Planning and Organizing

Being prepared will help you be successful. Being prepared is knowing what you need to do and when you need to do it. One way to accomplish this is with checklists.

Directions: Make a checklist to help you get ready for school in the morning. Write tasks in order from the first thing you do to the last. Use items from the list, or write your own.

brush my teeth	get dressed	pack my backpack
eat breakfast	get in the car	play with my sibling
feed your pet	get on the bus	take a shower

☐ _____

☐ _____

☐ _____

☐ _____

☐ _____

☐ _____

Directions: Create a different checklist that will help you during a different part of the day.

☐ _____

☐ _____

☐ _____

☐ _____

☐ _____

☐ _____

Name: _____ **Date:** _____

Getting What You Need

Your education is very important. One way you can make sure you get the most out of it is to speak up for yourself and say what you need.

Directions: Answer the questions to identify how each student can speak up for what they need.

Lucy has been struggling in math. She is behind on her assignments. She is worried about an upcoming exam.

1. What does Lucy need?

_____

_____

2. Who can she ask for help?

_____

_____

Kamaar has been getting teased at school. He is so worried about it that it's affecting his focus in class.

3. What does Kamaar need?

_____

_____

4. Who can he ask for help?

_____

_____

Directions: Describe a time when you needed to speak up for yourself. What did you need? Who helped you?

_____

_____

Name: _____ Date: _____

Focus on School

Relationship Skills

Peer Pressure

Peer pressure is when someone tries to make you do something that you know is wrong or that you do not want to do. It can be hard to say no or to stand up to others. But you will be able to do it if you have the right skills.

Directions: Read each situation. Write what you could do to help stop the peer pressure.

1. You are working on a group project. One person in your group tells you to do all the work and put everyone's name on the project. The person tells you they will invite you to play basketball at recess if you do.

   _____

   _____

   _____

2. You see some kids teasing another kid about the clothes they wear. They see you watching and yell for you to come join them.

   _____

   _____

   _____

Directions: Write about a time you stood up to peer pressure. How did it make you feel?

_____

_____

_____

_____

_____

_____

Name: _____ **Date:** _____

Solving Problems

You can be a problem solver. You can learn problem-solving skills by watching how other people react to problems they have.

Directions: Answer the questions about a problem you have seen at school.

1. Describe the problem. _____

    _____

    _____

2. How did the people involved try to solve the problem? _____

    _____

    _____

3. How would you have solved the problem? _____

    _____

    _____

Directions: Draw each step of how you would have solved the problem.

┌─────────────┐ ┌─────────────┐ ┌─────────────┐
│   │ │   │ │   │
│   │ │   │ │   │
│   │ │   │ │   │
│   │ │   │ │   │
│   │ │   │ │   │
└─────────────┘ └─────────────┘ └─────────────┘

Focus on School

Responsible Decision-Making

Name: _____ Date: _____

Focus on Community

Self-Awareness

Know How You Feel

Events in your community impact your emotions. Your emotions then impact your actions. It is like a chain. Your emotions and actions do not happen by themselves. They are both affected by things around them.

Directions: Write the missing piece in each reaction chain. Follow the example. Then, write your own reaction chain.

Example:

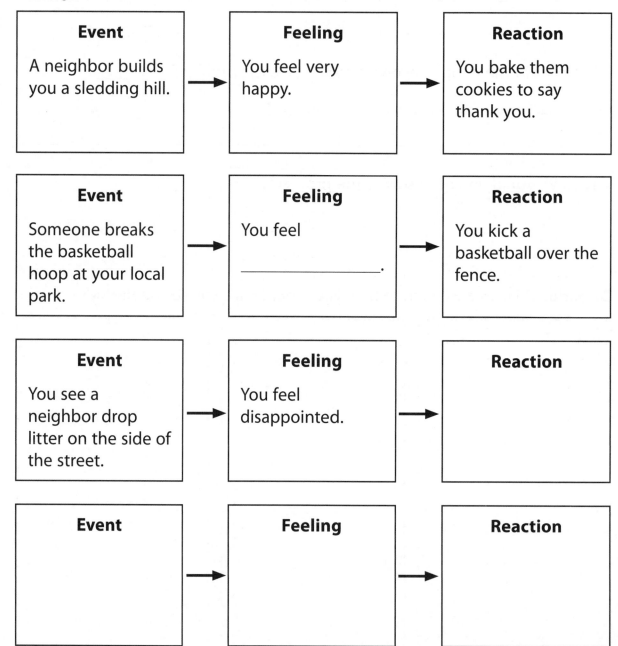

Event	**Feeling**	**Reaction**
A neighbor builds you a sledding hill.	You feel very happy.	You bake them cookies to say thank you.

Event	**Feeling**	**Reaction**
Someone breaks the basketball hoop at your local park.	You feel _____.	You kick a basketball over the fence.

Event	**Feeling**	**Reaction**
You see a neighbor drop litter on the side of the street.	You feel disappointed.	

Event	**Feeling**	**Reaction**

Name: _____ Date: _____

Trying New Things

Trying new things can be scary or overwhelming. Sometimes, it's hard to know how to start. We may worry that things will not work out or that we may fail. But if we don't find a way to overcome the fear, we will miss out on new things that we may love. It also can feel really good to overcome our fear.

Directions: Read the strategies for conquering your fear. Then, answer the questions.

How to Conquer Fear

- **I Can:** Say what you want to do out loud. Change the word *want* to *can*. For example, if you want to act in a community theater play, say, "I *CAN* act in a play!" This is a confident statement that says you believe in your abilities.

- **Just Imagine:** Picture yourself overcoming your fear. Professional athletes do this all the time. Imagine yourself doing whatever it is you want to do and doing it really well. If you want to act in the play, imagine the steps you will take to learn your lines. Imagine the audition for the play. Imagine how it will feel when you perform on opening night.

- **Look What I Did:** List similar things you have already done. If you are worried that you will be unable to accomplish your goal, think back to all the things you used to think were too hard. Did you learn to ride a bike? Make a new friend? Ace a test? Thinking about what you have overcome will help you feel confident that you can succeed again.

1. Write one new skill that you are nervous to try.

_____

2. Which of the three strategies could help you get started?

_____

3. Write how you will feel when you accomplish your goal.

_____

Focus on Community

Self-Management

Name: _____ Date: _____

Saying Thank You

Saying thank you for the nice things others do for you is a helpful way to build a strong community. It also feels good to tell someone you appreciate them.

Directions: Answer the questions.

1. List the helpers in your community who make it a nice place to live.

_____

_____

_____

_____

2. List ways you can thank the helpers.

_____

_____

_____

_____

3. Choose one person in your community to thank.

_____

4. Draw a picture showing how you will thank that person.

126961—180 Days of Social-Emotional Learning   © Shell Education

Name: _____ Date: _____

Solving Conflicts

When you are trying to solve a conflict, three things can happen. First, you could find a solution that pleases people on both sides of the conflict. This is called a win-win solution. Second, you could find a solution that pleases the person on one side of the conflict, but not the other. This is called a win-lose solution. Third, you could find a solution that pleases no one. This is called a lose-lose solution.

Directions: Draw a line to match each solution with the type of outcome.

Basketball Time

Megan and her friends are playing basketball at a local park. They have been playing for hours and do not want to stop. Josiah and Julian have been waiting for their turn to play on the court. They are getting frustrated.

All of the kids get into a fight and are sent home.	Win-Win
Megan and her friends stop so Josiah and Julian can play.	Win-Lose
Each group takes half of the court. They play at the same time.	Lose-Lose

Directions: On a separate sheet of paper, write an example of each type of solution to this problem.

You are at the corner store with your friend, and you both want to buy the same candy bar. There is only one left.

Focus on Community

Relationship Skills

Name: _____ **Date:** _____

Being Thoughtful

Being thoughtful and helping others will make your community a better place. It will make you feel good, too.

Directions: Write something under each picture that you could do to be thoughtful. Then, answer the question.

1.

_____

_____

3.

_____

_____

2.

_____

_____

4.

_____

_____

5. Think about your own neighborhood. Whom could you help? How could you be thoughtful?

_____

_____

_____

Name: _____ **Date:** _____

Identifying Bias

Bias happens when someone judges a person or group in an unfair way. Bias comes from opinions you might have about that person or group. Thinking girls can't play sports is a form of bias. Believing all people from a certain place are the same is also a bias. Everyone has some biases. It is important to recognize your own biases and the biases of others. That will help you keep your thoughts in check.

Directions: Read the texts, and answer the questions.

Zeke and Tony both want to play basketball. Zeke is very tall. Zeke has never played basketball before, but Tony assumes Zeke is the better player.

1. Who has a bias?

_____

Sheena has a really good singing voice. But she was not chosen for the play. The person who cast the play assumed she doesn't know how to sing.

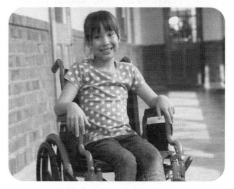

2. Who has a bias?

_____

Directions: Describe a time you have noticed bias. Include what happened and what the bias was.

_____

_____

_____

_____

_____

Focus on State

Self-Awareness

Name: _____ Date: _____

Focus on State
Self-Management

Personal and Collective Goals

Sometimes, you will need help from others to complete a goal. Having help while you are working on a goal can make it go faster, and it's a lot more fun!

Directions: Read the text, and answer the questions.

Sled Dogs to the Rescue

In 1925, the town of Nome, Alaska, needed a treatment for a disease. A disease called diphtheria was affecting children in the small town. It was winter, and there was no way to get medicine to the town. The people in the town made a plan. They decided to use dogsled teams to get the medicine. The distance was too far for one dogsled team to make it on their own. So, 20 teams worked together. Each ran as far as they could. Working together, 20 mushers and 150 dogs were able to get the medicine and save the town.

1. What was the goal in the dogsled run?

_____

2. Who got the diphtheria medicine to Nome?

_____

3. What might have happened if one person had tried to work alone?

_____

_____

4. What is a goal you have, and how could others help you complete it?

_____

_____

_____

_____

Name: _____ Date: _____

How Rules Can Be Unfair

Every state has laws that tell its citizens how to act. These laws are meant to be fair and keep everyone safe. But sometimes rules are unfair and need to be changed.

Directions: Read each law. Write whether the law is fair or unfair and why.

1. Everyone must drive under the speed limit.

_____

_____

2. Only girls can play volleyball in high school.

_____

_____

3. Everyone needs to throw litter in the trash.

_____

_____

4. Dogs are not allowed in the park without a leash.

_____

_____

Directions: Write a law that is fair and one that is unfair. Then, answer the question.

Fair Law: _____

Unfair Law: _____

5. How could you change the unfair law to be fairer?

_____

_____

Focus on State
Social Awareness

Name: _____ Date: _____

Focus on State

Relationship Skills

Offering Help to Others

Our community is strongest when we help each other. We can help each other by being kind or by lending a helping hand.

Directions: Describe how people in each picture are being helpful. Then, answer the question.

1.

_____

_____

3.

_____

_____

2.

_____

_____

4.

_____

_____

5. How can you be helpful in your state?

_____

_____

_____

Name: _____ Date: _____

Solving Problems

Did you ever wonder how your school gets money? Most schools are funded by the state government. This means that the state gives them money so they can pay for what they need. States fund schools so everyone can have the best education possible.

Directions: Write a letter to your governor or one of your state representatives. Tell them why they should fund schools. Include why school is important to you and what would happen if your school were not funded.

Dear _____,

_____

_____

_____

_____

_____

_____

_____

_____

_____

_____

_____

_____

_____

_____

Sincerely,

_____

Name: _____ Date: _____

Focus on Country

Self-Awareness

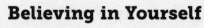

Believing in Yourself

It is up to you to follow your dreams. Many presidents, senators, civil rights activists, and other great leaders have had to work hard to accomplish their goals. Many of them had to deal with bullies and people who told them that they would not accomplish their dreams. But they persevered. If you believe in yourself, you can do great things, too.

Directions: Answer the questions.

1. If you could achieve anything you wanted, what would you do? Why?

   _____

   _____

   _____

2. Imagine someone telling you that you can't make that dream come true. What would you tell them? Remember to be strong and believe in yourself.

   _____

   _____

   _____

3. Draw yourself achieving your dream.

Name: _____ Date: _____

Practicing Self-Talk

Self-talk can help you get through tough times. If you practice positive self-talk, you can be ready to use it when you're in a tough spot. Self-talk can help you stay in a positive frame of mind and keep your focus strong.

Directions: Read each example. If it is positive self-talk, write *positive self-talk* on the line. If it is negative self-talk, rewrite it to be more positive.

1. I am never going to learn to ride my bike. I am going to have to use training wheels forever.

   _____

2. I am really struggling in my math class. But I think if I ask for extra help, I can figure it out.

   _____

3. My friend is a much better artist than me. But if I keep practicing, I know I can improve.

   _____

4. I keep forgetting my homework at home. I should just stop doing it.

   _____

5. I keep messing up my solo in band. I'll never get it right.

   _____

   _____

6. I keep missing my free throws. But I can get better if I practice some more.

   _____

   _____

Name: _____ Date: _____

Perspectives of Others

Have you ever had a disagreement with a friend? It is common to disagree with other people. But we can work to understand their perspectives. Doing this will help us find common ground and maintain our relationships.

Directions: Read the text, and answer the questions.

Forests

Forests are an important part of our world. They provide wood for building houses and making things we use daily, such as paper. They also provide oxygen to breathe and homes for wildlife. Many forests are protected by the U.S. government.

1. Explain why it is important to use trees.

_____

_____

2. Explain why it is important to save trees.

_____

_____

3. Seeing both sides of an issue will help you better understand the problem and come up with a solution. What common ground can both sides find on this issue?

_____

_____

4. Should the government continue protecting U.S. forests? Write an argument that would help others see your perspective.

_____

_____

Name: _____ **Date:** _____

Standing Up for Yourself

Hopefully, you have many people in your life who support you as you work toward your dreams. You may still meet someone who tries to tell you that you cannot do something. It is up to you to stand strong and believe in yourself.

Directions: Read the text. Then, write two endings to the story.

Singing Dilemma

Delaysia really wants to get a singing part in a play. She has tried out twice, but has not been cast in a part. She practices singing every day and is learning many new singing skills. Sean is in the theatre group. He told Delaysia she should stop trying. He thinks that if she were going to be cast in a play, it would have happened already.

1. Write the ending to this story if Delaysia listens to Sean.

_____

_____

_____

_____

_____

2. Write the ending to this story if Delaysia believes in herself.

_____

_____

_____

_____

_____

Name: _____ Date: _____

Focus on Country

Responsible Decision-Making

Prioritizing

When you get a job, you will pay taxes. Taxes are the money that the government takes out of your paycheck to pay for the needs of the country. People debate how tax money should be used. Congress and the president help decide how to use tax money. They need to prioritize, or decide what is most important, to spend this money wisely.

Directions: Imagine you are a member of Congress. You need to decide how to spend tax money. You might want to focus on things people need, such as researching new medicines. Or maybe you want to create a new national park. Or maybe you want to help protect the environment. List your priorities, and explain why each is important.

1. _____

_____

_____

2. _____

_____

_____

3. _____

_____

_____

4. _____

_____

_____

5. _____

_____

_____

Name: _____ **Date:** _____

Demonstrating Honesty

The internet is full of information. That is usually good, but it can also lead to dishonest behavior. It is important to be honest while using the internet.

Directions: Read the text, and answer the questions.

Last-Minute Report

You have a big report due tomorrow. You waited until the last minute. Now, you are trying to find information on the internet for your report. You come across an essay that is just like the one you should be writing. You consider just copying the essay and putting your name on it.

1. What is one reason you should not copy the essay?

_____

_____

2. What could be one consequence of copying the essay?

_____

_____

3. Why is it important to be honest when you are working online?

_____

_____

Directions: Draw a comic strip to show the honest thing to do in this situation.

Name: _____ Date: _____

Showing Self-Discipline

The internet is full of things to do. You can have a lot of fun, but you can also lose track of time and spend hours just playing around. Spending too much time online can cause problems in your social life. It can also give you a stiff neck!

Directions: Answer the questions about how you spend your time online.

1. What is one way you can monitor your time online?

   _____

   _____

2. What is one thing you can do if you are spending too much time online?

   _____

   _____

3. Name three things you can do instead of being on the internet.

   _____

   _____

   _____

4. Draw a picture of you doing one of those things.

Name: _____ Date: _____

Understanding Different Rules

Like many other places, the internet has its own set of rules. Some of these rules may be the same as your house's or your school's. Other rules may be different. These rules are put in place to keep you safe and to make sure you are able to have fun online.

Directions: List rules that people should follow while they are online.

Internet Safety Rules

1. _____
   _____

2. _____
   _____

3. _____
   _____

4. _____
   _____

5. _____
   _____

6. _____
   _____

Focus on Self

Social Awareness

Name: _____ Date: _____

Digital Communication

The internet has its own way of communicating. It has its own language! This means it also has its own challenges. It is important to understand the language of the internet. This will help you avoid its hazards.

Directions: Write what each abbreviation means. Check with a friend if you are not sure.

1. LOL _____

2. BRB _____

3. TTYL _____

4. IDK _____

Directions: Write what you would think if you received these messages. Then, answer the questions

5. WHERE ARE YOU? _____

_____

6. Can I *car* over to your house? _____

_____

7. Write your own message that could be confusing.

_____

_____

8. How can you help make sure that your messages are clear?

_____

_____

_____

Name: _____ **Date:** _____

Thinking about Your Actions

Your actions have consequences. It is easy to hide behind your computer when you are online. But there are consequences there, too. Just as in real life, you must make responsible decisions online.

Directions: Write a possible consequence of each action.

1. You are not allowed to take your tablet into your bedroom. Your family is not paying attention, so you sneak it in there before bed.

   _____

   _____

2. You find someone's phone. They are signed into their social media account. You find an embarrassing photo of them and post it as a joke.

   _____

   _____

3. You meet someone online while playing a game. They ask you for your real name and where you live. You give them your personal information.

   _____

   _____

Directions: Design a flyer explaining why it is important to make responsible decisions online.

Name: _____ Date: _____

Being Honest

It can be tempting to tell a little lie to get something you want. But when you are dishonest, people will lose trust in you. Honesty is important to keep your relationships strong.

Focus on Family
Self-Awareness

Directions: Read the text, and answer the questions.

While Naomi is cleaning, she bumps into a vase full of flowers. The vase falls to the floor and breaks. Naomi knows it's her mom's favorite vase, so she is afraid to tell her the truth. Naomi considers telling her mom that the dog broke the vase.

1. What is the honest choice?_____

_____

2. What might happen if Nomi chooses this?_____

_____

3. What is the dishonest choice?_____

_____

4. What might happen if Naomi chooses this?_____

_____

Directions: Think about a time when you could have chosen to tell the truth or tell a lie. Then, answer the questions.

5. Describe the situation. _____

_____

6. Did you choose to tell the truth or a lie? Why? _____

_____

7. If you were in a similar situation again, what would you do? Why?

_____

Name: _____ **Date:** _____

Calming Down

Many of us spend a lot of time with our families. We know them very well. We know what they like and what they don't like. Their opinions are valuable to us, and this is also why they can make us so angry! It's okay to get angry at the people we love. We just need to know how to calm our bodies when it happens.

Directions: Practice these three-step ways to help anger leave your body.

Stand up and follow these steps.

1. Do 10 really big jumping jacks.

2. Jump as high as you can five times.

3. Run in place for one minute.

How does your body feel? Do you feel calmer now that you moved your body?

Follow these steps. Go outside and try them if you are able.

1. Take a walk outside. It doesn't have to be far. Just walk in a big circle. Walk fast, then slowly, then fast again.

2. Do a couple quick sprints. Run as fast as you can for a short distance. Then, turn around and run back.

3. If you are alone outside, yell as loudly as you can.

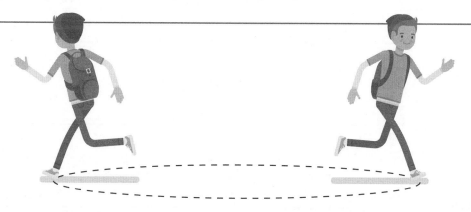

Name: _____ Date: _____

Focus on Family

Social Awareness

Finding Strengths of Others

Think about your family. Each person has different skills and strengths. Knowing your family members' strengths will improve your relationships with them.

Directions: Draw all the people in your family. Then, write about what each person does well. Add additional family members on another sheet of paper, if needed.

My Family

---

1. _____ is good at _____

_____.

2. _____ is good at _____

_____.

3. _____ is good at _____

_____.

4. _____ is good at _____

_____.

5. _____ is good at _____

_____.

Name: _____ Date: _____

Solving Problems

Having problems is a normal part of being in a family. You can't avoid conflicts and problems all the time. But you can be ready to solve problems when they occur.

Directions: Read the text. Then, complete the *ABCDE*s of this problem.

Weekend Mornings

Pete lives with his cousin, Shane. Pete likes to sleep in on the weekends after a long week at school. Shane gets up early on the weekends to watch his favorite TV shows. The noise from the TV wakes up Pete.

Ask: What is the problem?

1. _____

Brainstorm: What are some solutions?

2. _____

_____

_____

Choose: What is the best idea?

3. _____

Do: Make a plan.

4. _____

_____

_____

Evaluate: How will you know if the idea is successful?

5. _____

_____

Focus on Family
Relationship Skills

Name: _____ Date: _____

Focus on Family

Responsible Decision-Making

Helping Your Family

Everyone needs a helping hand every once in a while. You can help people in your family when they need to get things done. You can also help just to make them feel good.

Directions: Write the names of different people in your family. If you have a smaller family, include some extended family members or close friends. Write something you can do to help each person. Then, write how they might feel when you help them.

1. Family member: _____

   How you can help: _____

   How they will feel: _____

2. Family member: _____

   How you can help: _____

   How they will feel: _____

3. Family member: _____

   How you can help: _____

   How they will feel: _____

4. Family member: _____

   How you can help: _____

   How they will feel: _____

5. Family member: _____

   How you can help: _____

   How they will feel: _____

 126961—180 Days of Social-Emotional Learning

Name: _____ **Date:** _____

Handling Prejudice and Discrimination

Some people are judged based on their gender. Others are judged on the color of their skin or because they have a disability. Judging someone like this is called *prejudice*. Treating them unfairly is called *discrimination*.

Directions: Read the scenarios, and answer the questions.

The Sunnyside Pizza Company doesn't hire Sharissa for a job. Sharissa uses crutches to walk.

1. What prejudice might the Sunnyside Pizza Company have?

_____

_____

2. What discrimination might have happened?

_____

_____

Miguel is playing baseball with some friends in their neighborhood, and a girl wants to join. But some of the kids assume she can't play baseball.

3. What prejudice might some of the kids have?

_____

_____

4. What could Miguel do to help solve the situation?

_____

_____

Name: _____ Date: _____

Being an Ally

Being an ally means you stand with someone who needs support. Sometimes, it means standing up and taking action. Other times, it might just mean you stand beside them.

Focus on Community

Self-Management

Directions: Answer the questions.

1. You see someone getting teased for making a bad shot at basketball. How could you be an ally?

   _____

   _____

   _____

2. You see a kid from your school sitting alone on the swings. How could you be an ally?

   _____

   _____

   _____

3. Describe a time when someone needed your help or support.

   _____

   _____

   _____

4. What could you have done to be an even better ally?

   _____

   _____

   _____

Name: _____ Date: _____

The Feelings of Others

Being able to guess or predict what might happen because of your actions is an important skill. It will help you make good decisions and avoid doing things that hurt other people's feelings. You can choose to do things that help others feel better.

Directions: Read each scenario. Write *True* if the statement is likely true. Write *False* if the statement is likely false.

1. Alfie is reading a book. Alfie's friend tells him that the book is too easy and calls him a baby. Alfie feels proud.

   _____

2. Alang's friend just told him he is not a very good baseball player. Alang feels sad and hurt.

   _____

3. Rhonda and her friend are watching TV. Her friend starts talking about how much she likes the new girl at school. Rhonda feels jealous.

   _____

4. Kalia is playing on the playground. Two big kids near her start yelling and fighting. Kalia feels safe.

   _____

Directions: Circle one of the false statements. Then, write how the person might really feel.

_____

_____

_____

_____

Focus on Community

Social Awareness

Name: _____ Date: _____

Focus on Community

Relationship Skills

Communication Skills

Communication can be tricky. Even if you are actively listening, you can still miss a message. One way to make sure you are getting a message is to *paraphrase* it. This means you repeat the idea without repeating every word. You can also ask questions.

Directions: Paraphrase each message. Follow the example.

Example: Javier's mom says, "I want you to help out around the house. You need to take out the garbage and clean your room. Make sure you have it all done before our friends come over for dinner tonight."

Javier's response: _"I can take out the garbage and have my room clean before dinner. Is that all?"_

1. Olivia and her older sister Allie are getting off the school bus. They are still far from home. Olivia says, "Allie, please don't run ahead. Last time, I got scared and felt lost."

   Allie's response: _____

   _____

   _____

   _____

2. Gene is in math class. His teacher is explaining a tricky math problem. His teacher says, "Try the problem on your own. If you don't understand, ask your neighbor. If that doesn't work, then bring your work up to me. I will show you a different way to do it." Gene really does not understand the problem.

   Gene's response: _____

   _____

   _____

   _____

Solving Problems

Conflicts can happen in your family. They can happen with your friends. They can even happen in your community. A *compromise* is when both people give a little bit to help solve a conflict. You can compromise to help resolve conflicts in your community.

Directions: Read the text, and answer the questions.

The Noisy Building

A new building is going up in your neighborhood. The construction workers work hard from early in the morning until late at night. Your neighbors are frustrated because the noise wakes them up. Several neighbors try to get the company to stop the work.

1. What is the problem?

_____

_____

2. What do your neighbors want?

_____

_____

3. What does the construction company want?

_____

_____

4. What are two possible compromises?

_____

_____

_____

_____

Focus on Community

Responsible Decision-Making

Name: _____ **Date:** _____

Prejudice and Discrimination

Sometimes, people are treated unfairly. They are treated unfairly because of factors such as race or gender. This is prejudice. It can lead to discrimination. Both of these things are very harmful.

In 1954, the citizens of Topeka, Kansas, took on prejudice. They challenged the idea of segregated schools. At that time, Black students went to one school. White children went to another. Many people did not think this was right. They took their case to the Supreme Court. Their efforts led to the desegregation of all schools in the United States.

Directions: In 1960, Ruby Bridges was the first Black student to attend an all-white school. As she walked into school, people yelled at her. They told her to go back to her old school. Write a paragraph describing how Ruby Bridges might have felt on her first day at this new school.

Setting Up Group Goals

Sometimes, problems are so big that you need help to solve them. When that happens, people of all skills can come together to work on a goal. When everyone works together, they can achieve their goals.

Directions: Imagine a state park near you has been damaged by a big storm. You want to work with others to clean it up. Set up your goal by answering the questions.

1. How long will the cleanup take?

_____

2. Who can help clean up the park?

_____

3. What supplies will you need?

_____

_____

4. What setbacks might you encounter?

_____

_____

5. How might you solve them?

_____

_____

_____

6. How will you know when your goal is achieved?

_____

_____

Focus on State
Self-Management

Name: _____ Date: _____

Focus on State

Social Awareness

How to Act in Different Groups

You need to act differently in different places. The rules at your home might be different than the rules at school. When you learn how to change your behavior based on where you are, you will feel more comfortable.

Directions: Write the behavior that is expected in each location.

	Voice Level loud/quiet/both	Running yes/no/ sometimes	Roughhousing yes/no/ sometimes	Shoes on/off/both
home				
school				
library				
museum				
playground				

Directions: What other places around your state have their own rules? Write two more locations and their rules.

1. _____

_____

_____

_____

2. _____

_____

_____

_____

Traits of a Good Leader

Your state is full of leaders. The governor is the primary state leader. Being a leader takes a lot of hard work. Knowing what skills are important to have will help you be a good leader and choose your leaders wisely.

Directions: Circle the traits and skills that a good leader should have.

arrogant	genius	popular
athletic	hard worker	reliable
calm under pressure	helps others	rich
critical thinker	kind	sets goals
empathetic	listens to others	speaks from the heart
enthusiastic	loud	talkative
focused	passionate	trustworthy

Focus on State
Relationship Skills

Directions: Answer the questions.

1. Write the leadership traits and skills that you have.

_____

_____

_____

_____

2. How could you use your traits and skills to make your state a better place?

_____

_____

_____

_____

Name: _____ Date: _____

Making a Difference

There are many great organizations that work to make a difference. Most of them are meant for adult volunteers. But did you know that you can make a difference, too? Volunteering is not just for adults. It's also for kids!

Directions: Follow the steps to determine how you could volunteer in your state.

1. Who in your state might need a helping hand? Write as many people or groups as you can.

   _____

   _____

   _____

2. What skills and interests do you have that would be the most helpful? Write as many as you can.

   _____

   _____

   _____

Directions: In the first box, write one person or group who could use your help. In the second box, write one of your skills or interests that could help them. In the third box, write a way both those things could come together.

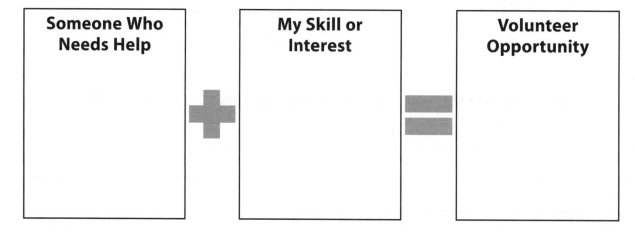

Someone Who Needs Help	My Skill or Interest	Volunteer Opportunity

Name: _____ Date: _____

Standing Up for Your Needs

Being able to stand up for your needs is an important skill. When challenges happen, you need to be able to *advocate* for the things you need. To advocate is to fight for a cause or a belief.

Directions: Write how each person can advocate for themself and ask for what they need.

1. Christina is having a hard time with math. She doesn't understand what is being taught, and she has a big test coming up. She asked a friend for help, but she still doesn't understand the material.

   _____

   _____

2. Max is being teased at school. He is scared to go to recess because the kids are threatening to beat him up. He told the recess monitor, but they told him to just go play somewhere else.

   _____

   _____

Directions: Write about a time when you advocated for yourself. Draw the outcome.

_____

_____

Name: _____ Date: _____

Managing Disappointment

Everyone experiences disappointment. It can be difficult when you try hard and still fail. But the way you respond to failure makes all the difference.

Directions: Complete these sentences about your strengths and amazing abilities.

I am _____.

I can _____.

I know _____.

I feel _____.

I will _____.

Directions: Repeat this sentence in your head three times. Then, describe how you feel.

When I fall down, I will get back up. I believe in me!

_____

_____

_____

Name: _____ **Date:** _____

The Feelings of Others

It's important to understand the feelings of other people. When you know how people are feeling, you will better know how to help them.

Focus on Country

Social Awareness

Directions: Read each scenario. Explain how each person is feeling and what their friend could do to help them feel better.

1. Tina and Rhonda have worked really hard all year to make the cheerleading team. They both practiced every day for the last month. After tryouts, Rhonda did not make the team, but Tina did.

   _____

   _____

   _____

2. Juan is running for class president. He is running against two classmates. When the election is over, the teacher announces that Juan won.

   _____

   _____

   _____

3. Marcy just voted for the first time. The person she voted for did not win. Her friend, Terry, voted for the person who won.

   _____

   _____

   _____

4. Liam has been working really hard on his science fair project. On the day of the fair, his project doesn't work, and he is devastated. His friend, Jordan, is also at the science fair, and her robot is the talk of the school.

   _____

   _____

   _____

Name: _____ **Date:** _____

Standing Up for Others

You have a voice, and you can use it to stand up for the rights of others. You can also use your voice to stand by people who need support. You can even use your voice to tell your leaders what kinds of laws and policies you want them to create. Your voice is powerful!

Directions: Write a letter to one of your elected officials about an issue that is important to you. Tell them why the issue is important to you. Include facts and how the issue makes you feel.

Dear _____ ,

_____

_____

_____

_____

_____

_____

_____

_____

_____

_____

_____

_____

Sincerely,

_____

Name: _____ Date: _____

Solving Problems

No matter the size of a problem, you can use the same steps to find a solution. Even when a problem is huge, it's important to first understand the situation. Then, you can find a solution.

A gas rig exploded in the Gulf of Mexico in 2010. It caused an oil spill that hurt local wildlife. Federal and local governments worked together. They asked questions. They learned about the problem. Then, they thought of solutions. They worked together to save as much wildlife as they could.

Directions: Choose one of these problems, and plan a solution.

Problems

- Your school is supposed to have a picnic at a local park. But a recent storm flooded the picnic area.

- Your community needs a new fire truck. But it doesn't have the money to buy one on its own.

- The kids in your town want to borrow books. But your library is closed for a month.

1. Which problem did you choose? _____

2. What questions do you need answered to solve this problem?

_____

_____

3. List three possible solutions.

- _____

- _____

- _____

4. Circle the best solution.

Name: _____ Date: _____

Connecting Feelings to Actions

Knowing what makes you happy, angry, or sad will help you make good choices. When you know what makes you angry or sad, you know what to avoid. When you know what makes you happy, you know what to look for when you need to cheer up.

Directions: List three things that make you feel each emotion. Be as descriptive as you can.

Happy

- _____

- _____

- _____

Angry

- _____

- _____

- _____

Sad

- _____

- _____

- _____

Directions: Circle one thing from the *Angry* category. Write two ways you could calm your body when this thing happens to you.

_____

_____

_____

Name: _____ Date: _____

Finding Triggers

A *trigger* is something that makes you really mad. If you know your triggers, you can avoid situations where you might find them. If your triggers do get pushed, you can be ready with some positive self-talk or calming skills.

Directions: Write a star next to the things that trigger you.

someone yelling at you	someone being a bully	someone telling you what to do	someone telling you to calm down
people taking your things without asking	someone saying something mean about your friends or family	not being able to figure out a tough problem	someone bragging about themselves
someone getting in your face	someone making fun of you	someone being super competitive	a friend who is always late

Directions: Circle one trigger you starred. Then, write two positive self-talk sentences you could use when you encounter this trigger again.

1. _____

_____

_____

2. _____

_____

_____

Name: _____ Date: _____

Focus on Self

Social Awareness

The Feelings of Others

Just like you, other people will sometimes make mistakes. It can be hard for people to own up to their mistakes and apologize. One thing you can do to help is to be aware of their feelings and be supportive when they try to make things right.

How to Accept an Apology

1. Look them in the eye. Use your body language to show you are open to hearing what they have to say.

2. If you are still really mad, take some deep breaths.

3. Repeat to yourself that everyone makes mistakes. You are glad they are owning up to theirs.

4. Accept their apology sincerely. Saying, "It's okay" is not enough. Tell them you are thankful for the apology. Use an I-message if you need to talk more about how you are feeling.

Directions: Write your response to this apology. Include both your words and your actions.

"I am really sorry that I broke your phone. I didn't mean to break it. I just wanted to take a picture, and it slipped. I feel really bad and will do whatever I can to make it right. I am so sorry. I hope we can still be friends."

_____

_____

_____

_____

_____

_____

Name: _____ Date: _____

Solving Conflicts

Solving conflicts when someone is angry can be tough. It can be hard to have a conversation when there are big feelings involved. But it will be worth it. Solving conflicts with people can make your relationships stronger.

Directions: Read the scenario. Role-play this conflict with a partner. Take turns being on both sides. Follow the steps each time.

Movie Watching

You and your friend were supposed to go to a movie together. You had been looking forward to seeing this movie for months. You were at your grandma's house the weekend of the movie premiere. When you came back, you found out that your friend saw the movie without you.

1. Use I-messages. Tell them how you feel using *I feel…when…I need…*.

2. Use positive self-talk. Give yourself a pep talk in your head to cool down.

3. Listen to their apology. Be a good listener. They may have a good reason for what they did.

4. Brainstorm a solution. Is there anything that could make this situation better?

Directions: Write a reflection about how the exercise went. Include how you felt about sharing your feelings and whether you found a solution.

_____

_____

_____

_____

_____

_____

Name: _____ Date: _____

Being Able to Say Sorry

Saying sorry can be tough to do. But the good news is you can get better with practice! Admitting you are wrong is hard and can be embarrassing, but you will feel so much better after you do!

Directions: Read the scenarios, and answer the questions.

You are playing basketball with a group of friends. You are feeling really good and want to show off your new moves. As you dribble towards the basket, you push a friend out of the way. You didn't mean to be so rough, but your friend falls to the ground and twists their ankle.

1. What self-talk could you use to help you calm down?

_____

_____

2. What could you say and do for your friend?

_____

_____

You don't know where your textbook is, so you borrow your friend's book two days before a big test. You promise to bring it back so they will also have time to study. But then you find out that your dog tore up the book. The book is destroyed, and your friend is really upset.

3. What self-talk could you use to help you calm down?

_____

_____

4. What could you say and do for your friend?

_____

_____

Name: _____ **Date:** _____

Feelings Check-In

Life can get pretty busy. Sometimes, it is easy to forget to check in with how you are feeling. When we disconnect from our feelings, we can get overwhelmed or tense without knowing why. If this happens to you, you can reconnect your mind and body with a simple check-in.

1. Take a deep breath.

2. Notice how your body feels. Are you tense? Does your stomach or head hurt?

3. Ask your brain what it is thinking. Is it worried about anything?

4. Now, connect how your body feels to what your brain is thinking.

Directions: Write about a time when you could have used a feelings check-in. Describe what happened. Explain how a check-in would have helped. Then, draw yourself using a feelings check-in.

_____

_____

_____

_____

Name: _____ **Date:** _____

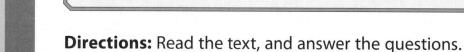

Learning How to Lose with Grace

Losing can be hard to handle. It can make you feel angry, sad, or frustrated. With practice, you can learn how to lose gracefully. When you are able to do that, everyone will have a lot more fun, and you'll feel better, too.

Directions: Read the text, and answer the questions.

Playing Cards

Kris is playing a card game with Cassie. Kris is ahead until the last hand, when Cassie suddenly wins. Kris can choose to lose gracefully. He could thank Cassie for the good game and tell her that he had fun playing. Or he could be a sore loser. Kris could get really frustrated and yell that Cassie must have cheated.

1. How do you think Kris felt after he lost the game? _____

_____

2. How might Kris feel if he loses gracefully? _____

_____

3. How might Cassie feel if Kris loses gracefully? _____

_____

4. How might Kris feel if he yells at Cassie? _____

_____

5. How might Cassie feel if Kris yells at her? _____

_____

6. How might Cassie help Kris handle the loss? _____

_____

Focus on Friends / Self-Management

Name: _____ Date: _____

Finding Ways to Thank Your Friends

It is a gift to have friends in your life. It can be fun finding ways to thank them. You can do this in many ways. You can thank them with words, you can make them something, or you can do something nice for them. Thanking your friends can make your friendships even stronger.

Directions: Write the names of two friends who have done something nice for you. Write what each friend did and how you could thank them.

Friend's name: _____

What they did: _____

_____

How to thank them: _____

_____

Friend's name: _____

What they did: _____

_____

How to thank them: _____

_____

Directions: Draw yourself thanking one of those friends.

Name: _____ Date: _____

Strength in Teamwork

Have you ever wondered why it is easier to get things done when you are working together with other people? When we work with a team, we get to use everyone's strengths to get the job done. We all have different strengths, and when we put them together, our team is stronger!

Focus on Friends

Relationship Skills

Directions: In the first column, write an *X* next to your strengths. Write two friends' names at the top of the other two columns. Write an *X* next to each of their strengths. Then, answer the questions.

	Me		
being a good friend			
singing			
giving high fives			
reading			
telling jokes			
being kind to animals			
drawing			
playing sports			
playing video games			

1. Which skill is your weakest?

_____

2. How could someone else help you improve in that skill?

_____

_____

Name: _____ Date: _____

Thinking about Your Actions

It can be easy to forget that actions have consequences. If you act without thinking, you could hurt someone's feelings. Even if you say sorry, you might not be able to fix what you did.

Fold a sheet of paper in half. Make a good crease. Now, unfold the paper and try to smooth it out. The crease is like your actions. Even if you are really sorry, your actions will never fully go away. This is why it's important to stop and think about your actions.

Directions: Think about a time when your actions affected other people. Answer the questions. Then, draw how you can be mindful of your actions.

1. What did you do? _____

_____

2. How did the other person feel? _____

_____

3. Were you able to fix what you did? Why or why not?

_____

_____

4. What would you do differently if something similar happened again?

_____

_____

Responsible Decision-Making

Focus on Friends

Name: _____ Date: _____

Identifying Your Feelings

Things around you impact your feelings. Your home, school, and community can all make you feel many emotions.

Focus on Community

Self-Awareness

Directions: Think about the space where you are now (home, school, library, etc.). Write one thing from that space that fits each category.

Something that makes you laugh	Something you don't like
Something that makes you miss someone	Something that makes you nervous
Something that surprises you	Something that makes you happy
Something you could do with a friend	Something you would like to do alone
Something that makes you feel safe	Something that makes you excited
Something you could do somewhere else	Something you could do all day

Name: _____ Date: _____

Cooling Down When You Are Angry

Our environment can impact our feelings. It is good to know places in your community where you feel calm and safe. It is helpful to know where you can go when you are angry or just need a break.

Directions: Draw two places in your community where you feel safe. Explain why each place helps you feel calm.

```
┌─────────────────────────────────────────────┐
│                                             │
│                                             │
│                                             │
│                                             │
│                                             │
└─────────────────────────────────────────────┘
```

_____

_____

```
┌─────────────────────────────────────────────┐
│                                             │
│                                             │
│                                             │
│                                             │
│                                             │
└─────────────────────────────────────────────┘
```

_____

_____

Focus on Community

Self-Management

Name: _____ Date: _____

Acting Differently

We talk about and share different things with different people. For example, you can say different things to a friend than to a stranger. Learning this difference will help you understand what to talk about in social situations.

Directions: Write a topic you could talk about with each person. Write a topic you should not talk about with each person. Then, answer the questions.

People	Topics I Can Talk About	Topics I Shouldn't Talk About
parent		
friend		
grandparent		
teacher		
person at the grocery store		

1. Whom can you talk to about anything?

_____

2. Why is it so easy to talk to that person?

_____

_____

_____

Name: _____ **Date:** _____

Developing Positive Relationships

Many people have role models, or people they admire. When you see a role model make good decisions, you can model your own decisions based on what you learn from them. You may have role models in your home or in your school. You may also find role models in your community.

Directions: Draw a person who is a role model in your community. Then, write three reasons you look up to that person.

My role model is: _____

_____

_____

_____

Focus on Community

Relationship Skills

Name: _____ **Date:** _____

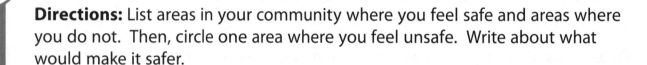

Help Your Community

Everyone wants to live in a safe place. Community members can work together to make that happen.

Directions: List areas in your community where you feel safe and areas where you do not. Then, circle one area where you feel unsafe. Write about what would make it safer.

Safe	Unsafe

_____

_____

_____

_____

126961—180 Days of Social-Emotional Learning   © Shell Education

Name: _____ **Date:** _____

Benefits of Where You Live

Every state is unique, and every state has things that make it a great place to live. Some states have big, bustling cities, while others have wide open spaces. Your state might have fun places to go, such as museums or amusement parts. Or it might have peaceful lakes and rivers. Or it might have warm, sunny beaches. Appreciating your state can help you love where you live.

Directions: Answer the questions. Look up facts and locations online if needed.

1. What fun things are there to do in your state?

_____

_____

2. What kinds of natural features does your state have?

_____

_____

3. What do you love about your state?

_____

_____

4. Draw a picture showing why your state is a great place to grow up.

Name: _____ **Date:** _____

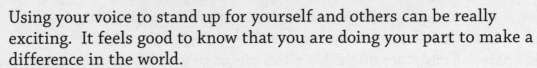

Standing Up for Yourself and Others

Using your voice to stand up for yourself and others can be really exciting. It feels good to know that you are doing your part to make a difference in the world.

Directions: Read the text. Then, write a letter to a member of your state legislature in support of one side of this issue. Tell them how this issue affects you and what you think they should do.

Late Start

Imagine your state is discussing changing school hours. Some people want school to start later in the day to let kids sleep in. They think this will help them miss fewer days of school. But other people have pointed out that the change would mean that students are in school until dinnertime. That leaves no room for afternoon activities, such as clubs, sports, and music.

_____

_____

_____

_____

_____

_____

_____

_____

_____

The Feelings of Others

It can be easy to forget that other people see things differently. When we feel strongly about an idea, it can be hard to see things as others do. But we are a country of different people with many different views. It is helpful to look at situations from all sides.

Focus on State

Social Awareness

Directions: Write the pros and cons for this state law. Write at least five examples for each side. Then, answer the question.

State Law: It is illegal to use a cell phone while driving. This includes making calls, texting, or using the internet.

Pros	Cons

1. How did stepping away from your own thinking change your views?

_____

_____

_____

Name: _____ Date: _____

Focus on State

Relationship Skills

How to Disagree and Stay Kind

Do you and your friends agree on everything? Do you have all the same ideas, likes, and dislikes? Probably not. We all have our own ideas, so it is normal to disagree with our friends or family. It is important to learn how to disagree with someone in a kind way.

How to Disagree Kindly

• Keep the conversation on-topic. Don't bring in other topics.

• Use I-messages to share your thoughts.

• Listen to the other person's point of view.

• Stay calm. Take a deep breath if you are getting heated.

Directions: Imagine your friend just told you that she thinks there should be school in the summer. You do not agree with her. You are feeling anxious at the idea of losing your summer break. Write three things you could say to share your point of view in a kind and respectful way.

1. _____

_____

_____

2. _____

_____

_____

3. _____

_____

_____

Name: _____ **Date:** _____

Keeping People Safe

Staying safe is very important. But how do you know how to stay safe? Sometimes, information changes, and we need to learn new ways to stay safe.

Governments need quick ways to tell people how to stay safe. They can post quick messages with easy directions. These are called Public Safety Announcements (PSAs). They may remind people of a safety issue or give new information.

Directions: Draw a PSA poster for a safety issue that people should know. It should include a picture and text to tell people how to stay safe.

My PSA Topic: _____

Name: _____ Date: _____

Being Honest

Being honest means telling the truth. It can be hard to be honest when you think you might get into trouble or you feel embarrassed about something that happened. But it feels better to be honest than to get away with a lie.

Our nation's 16th president, Abraham Lincoln, was known for being honest. His nickname was Honest Abe. Honesty is not just something we are born with. Even Honest Abe had to learn how.

Directions: Read the scenario, and answer the questions.

The Missing Wallet

Jamal and Zach are at the park. They find a wallet with money in it. They are excited because they want to use the money to buy snacks on their walk home. A little while later, a man comes by and asks them if they have seen a wallet. He lost his, and he is looking for it. Zach immediately tells the man no, but Jamal hesitates. The man looks at Jamal and is waiting for an answer.

1. What is the honest thing for Jamal to do? _____

_____

2. How would Jamal feel if he kept the money? _____

_____

3. How would Jamal feel if he gave the wallet back? _____

_____

4. What could Jamal say to Zach to convince him that they need to give the wallet back?

_____

_____

Name: _____ Date: _____

Setting Goals

One great way to achieve the things you want is to set goals. Some people like to write their goals and place them where they can see them every day. Writing your goals will help clarify what you want to accomplish. Looking at them every day can help remind you of your goals and keep you motivated.

Directions: Answer the questions to help you set two goals.

Goal: _____

When do you want to accomplish this goal?

_____

What steps will you take to accomplish your goal?

- _____
- _____
- _____

Whose help do you need to accomplish your goal?

_____

Goal: _____

When do you want to accomplish this goal?

_____

What steps will you take to accomplish your goal?

- _____
- _____
- _____

Whose help do you need to accomplish your goal?

_____

Focus on Country

Self-Management

Name: _____ Date: _____

Focus on Country

Social Awareness

Things Can Change How You Act and Feel

Many restaurants have to share the calorie content of their food. The goal is to help Americans eat better. The government hopes to change how people act by giving them more information.

Directions: Answer the questions about your favorite restaurant.

1. What is your favorite restaurant?

_____

2. What food do you order?

_____

3. What if you learned that your favorite food is low in nutrition? Would you still order it?

_____

4. Do you think that it is a good idea for the government to require restaurants to post nutrition information? Why or why not?

_____

_____

_____

5. What other actions might cause you to change how you act (either at a restaurant or somewhere else)?

_____

_____

_____

_____

_____

Name: _____ Date: _____

Standing Up for Yourself and Others

Someday, you may come across something that is just wrong. You will know in your heart that something must be done. It can be easy to sit back and wait for someone else to fix it, but if you do that, nothing may happen. It is up to you to stand up for the rights of yourself and others.

On average, women in the United States earn less than men who have the same job and experience. One group that is fighting to change this is the United States Women's National Soccer Team. They think it is unfair that they earn less than the men's team, even though they have won more championships. As they fight for equal pay, they play hard and win games.

Directions: Draw yourself standing up for something. Write dialogue using speech bubbles to show what you could say.

Name: _____ Date: _____

Focus on Country

Responsible Decision-Making

Helping Your Country

You can be a part of the change in your country. You just have to look for how you can help others and make things better.

John Lewis saw that Black Americans like him were being treated poorly because of the color of their skin. Lewis worked hard to fight this racism. Lewis went to marches and protests to help change the country for the better.

Directions: One way people help their countries is by raising awareness of things they want to change. Read the examples of messages. Then, make a sign to support something that would make the country better. Include a message and pictures.

Examples:

Support our veterans!

Save the environment!

Name: _____ **Date:** _____

Identifying Your Strengths

We all have strengths and weaknesses. Your strengths can be different from your friends' and family members' strengths.

Directions: Answer the questions to show how you can share your strengths with others.

1. What things are you good at (sports, arts, activities, helping others, or something else)?

   _____

   _____

   _____

2. Choose one strength that you could share with someone else. Why did you choose this strength?

   _____

   _____

   _____

3. With whom could you share this?

   _____

4. How could you share your strength with them?

   _____

   _____

   _____

   _____

Focus on Self

Self-Awareness

Name: _____ **Date:** _____

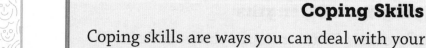

Coping Skills

Coping skills are ways you can deal with your emotions. Some coping skills are helpful, but some are not. Having a set of helpful coping skills will allow you to better handle your emotions and make sure they don't get away from you.

Directions: Sort the coping skills into the chart.

Helpful Coping Skills	Not Helpful Coping Skills

count to 10	roll your eyes	take a break
draw a picture	scream	take a deep breath
positive self-talk	slam a door	take a walk
punch a wall	storm off	talk to a friend
read a book	sulk	throw things

Name: _____ Date: _____

The Feelings of Others

People give us a lot of clues about how they are feeling. Even if you don't talk to someone, you can often learn their mood from their body language.

Focus on Self

Social Awareness

Directions: Write the feelings you see in each person's body language. Outline each person in a color that shows their mood. Then, draw yourself in a color that shows your mood. Write what you are feeling.

1.

_____

_____

_____

3.

_____

_____

_____

2.

_____

_____

_____

4.

_____

_____

_____

Name: _____ Date: _____

Focus on Self

Relationship Skills

Making Good Friends

It can be hard to make friends when you are in a new place. But it is a skill that you can learn with a little practice. Having this skill will help you feel comfortable making new friends.

How to Make a Friend

1. Smile and say hello.

2. Introduce yourself. Ask their name.

3. Ask questions about who they are or what they are doing.

4. Be brave, and ask if you can join them in what they are doing.

5. Ask if they want to do something with you.

Directions: Write a short story where one character makes friends with another. Be sure to include all five steps.

_____

_____

_____

_____

_____

_____

_____

_____

_____

_____

_____

_____

_____

How You Impact Others

When words come out of your mouth, you can't take them back. The best thing to do is to think before you speak.

THINK

Is it **T**rue?

Is it **H**elpful?

Is it **I**nspiring?

Is it **N**ecessary?

Is it **K**ind?

Directions: Read the scenario, and answer the questions.

The Drawing

August finishes a drawing that he has been working on for a long time. He is really excited to show it to his friend Ruthie. When Ruthie sees the drawing, she thinks that August used too much color and that it would have looked better if it wasn't so bright. Ruthie stops. Before she tells August this, she THINKs.

1. What could Ruthie say to August?

_____

_____

_____

2. Write how it fits the THINK categories.

True _____

Helpful _____

Inspiring _____

Necessary _____

Kind _____

Name: _____   Date: _____

Focus on School

Self-Awareness

Having a Growth Mindset

Having a growth mindset will help you overcome challenges. This means that your mind is open to new things. If your mindset is fixed, you will not move forward with your goals. The good news is that with some work, you can change your mindset from fixed to growth.

Directions: Rewrite each of the statements to show a growth mindset. Follow the example.

Example

This project is impossible. I should just give up.

This project is hard. But if I break it into small steps, I can do it.

1. I am not good at math. I never will be!

_____

2. Art is so hard. I am not an artist.

_____

3. Making friends is hard. I guess I will just eat lunch by myself.

_____

4. I didn't make the basketball team. I am just not good enough. I will never catch up to my friends.

_____

5. Skiing is so hard. I'll never move beyond the bunny hill.

_____

6. Why am I learning piano? My fingers don't work this way.

_____

Name: _____ **Date:** _____

Trying New Things

Trying new things can be scary, but if you don't try new things, you may never know what you could do. Trying new things at school could help you find a subject you are good at or a sport you love.

Directions: Answer the questions about something new you would like to try. If you need ideas, choose one from the list.

New Things to Try

advanced math	creative writing
art class	service club
band	sports
chess club	theater
choir	tutoring others

1. What do you want to try?

_____

2. How do you feel about trying this new thing?

_____

_____

3. Make a plan to try the new thing you chose. How can you make it less scary? Who might be able to help you?

_____

_____

_____

_____

_____

© Shell Education

Focus on School

Self-Management

Name: _____ Date: _____

Show Concern for Others

Be kind to others when you can. Being kind and showing concern for others will feel good, both for them and for you. When you are at school, you may see people who really need someone to be kind to them. You can be that person, and it can make a huge difference for them.

Directions: Write how you could be kind to each of these people.

1. A kid was left out of a game.

_____

_____

2. A kid was picked last for a sport at recess.

_____

_____

3. A girl is teased because she doesn't wear nice clothes.

_____

_____

4. A boy is teased because he doesn't like sports.

_____

_____

5. A boy gets left out because he talks with an accent.

_____

_____

6. A kid sits alone at lunch.

_____

_____

Saying No to Friends

Friends are an important part of our lives. It is normal to want your friends to like you. But sometimes, you will need to be able to say no to your friends, even if they get upset about it.

How to Say No

1. Be clear. Say no firmly but respectfully.

2. Be kind. You are saying no to what they are doing, not to their friendship.

3. Say how you feel without blaming anyone.

Directions: Read the scenarios. Write what each person could say or do to follow each step of saying no. Then, write about a time you had to say no to a friend or classmate.

1. Isaac forgot to do his homework. Now it is time to turn it in, and Isaac asks Damien if he can copy his answers.

_____

_____

_____

2. Grace wants to borrow Sarah's phone. But Sarah's parents got it for her and told her not to loan it to anyone.

_____

_____

_____

3. _____

_____

_____

Name: _____ Date: _____

Focus on School

Responsible Decision-Making

Solve Conflicts

With the right skills, you can solve problems for yourself and others. Helping others come up with solutions for their problems is a way you can help your friends and classmates.

Directions: Write how you could help resolve each conflict.

1. Two kids in your class want to read the same book during independent reading time. They try to find a similar book for one of them to read. But there is nothing else like it in their classroom library.

   _____

   _____

2. Some kids are playing soccer at recess. The game is really competitive. One kid kicks the ball really hard, and it hits another kid in the face. It was an accident, but the injured kid is angry.

   _____

   _____

Directions: Draw what one of the scenarios would look like after the conflict was resolved.

Name: _____ **Date:** _____

Personal Strengths

You are good at so many things. Your neighbors have many strengths, too. You can all use your unique strengths to contribute to your community.

Directions: Imagine your community is having a celebration. Everyone will bring something to eat and something to do. The things they bring will show their strengths. Write what you will bring to show your personal strengths.

1. Food: _____

2. Activity: _____

. . . .

Directions: Draw the celebration. Include your food and activity. Include a friend's contributions, too.

Name: _____ **Date:** _____

Managing Emotions

If you tune into your community, you may find that it can help you manage your emotions. Does your community have places that make you feel calm? Maybe it's a quiet park, or even a busy sidewalk. Your community can help you feel calm and safe if you look for it.

Directions: Use your senses to find places in your community that help you feel calm and safe.

1. Open your eyes. Then, write something you SEE in your community that helps you feel calm and safe.

_____

_____

_____

2. Open your ears. Then, write something you HEAR in your community that helps you feel calm and safe.

_____

_____

_____

3. Scrunch your nose. Then, write something you SMELL in your community that helps you feel calm and safe.

_____

_____

_____

4. Rub your hands together. Then, write something you FEEL in your community that helps you feel calm and safe.

_____

_____

_____

Name: _____ Date: _____

Taking Chances

Taking chances can be scary. Sometimes, you are not sure what will happen if you take a chance. One thing you can do is take a deep breath and think about all the possible outcomes. Knowing what the possible outcomes are might help you make a decision.

Directions: Read the text. List the good things that could happen on the left side of the seesaw. List the bad things that could happen on the right side. Then, answer the question.

Taking a Chance

Veronica likes to sing. She is so good at it that her teacher asks her to be the lead in a school play. Veronica does not know anything about acting, so her first thought is to say no. But then, she remembers that taking chances could lead to something exciting.

Good   **Bad**

1. If you were Veronica's friend, what would you tell her to do? Why?

_____

_____

Name: _____ Date: _____

Focus on Community

Relationship Skills

Seeking Help When You Need It

Your community can help when you are in need. Do you know who to go to in your community when you need help? You can find different people based on what your need is.

Directions: Write people in your community who could help you. You may write the same person for more than one answer.

1. I would go see _____ if I needed a safe place to be.

2. I would go see _____ if I needed someone to listen to me.

3. I would go see _____ if I needed advice.

4. I would go see _____ if I needed someone to cheer me up.

Directions: Circle one person. Write a thank you note to that person. Describe how they help you.

_____

_____

_____

_____

_____

_____

_____

_____

_____

_____

_____

How You Can Help

Community members take care of one another. They come together when someone is in need. They lend a hand when the community wants to change. One example of this is when people create a community watch program. This is a program where all neighbors keep an eye out to keep each other safe.

Directions: Your neighbors have decided to form a community watch. Brainstorm some ways you can help the new community watch. Then, draw a sign for your community watch. It should let others know that your community is committed to safety.

_____

_____

_____

_____

Name: _____ Date: _____

Identify Your Strengths

You will be able to get a driver's license when you are 16. Your driver's license lets you drive a car. It is also an identification card. It includes your address and your physical features. Imagine you are about to get your license, except this license lists your interests and strengths. Knowing your strengths helps you know how to respond to situations.

Directions: Complete your license. Write your state's name at the top, and draw your picture. Then, write the other information about yourself.

_____

NAME: _____

BIRTHDATE: _____

STRENGTHS:

_____

_____

_____

HOBBIES:

_____

_____

_____

DISLIKES:

_____

_____

_____

Name: _____ **Date:** _____

Planning Help

One role of state government is to help people. States offer services and provide resources to people in need. They build roads, maintain bridges, make sure traffic lights are working, and much more. To do this, states have to be very organized and have plans for how to keep everything moving forward.

Directions: Write a checklist of tasks you do to help out at home. Then, make a second checklist of big projects that you would like to do.

Task Checklist

☐ _____

☐ _____

☐ _____

☐ _____

☐ _____

Big Project Checklist

☐ _____

☐ _____

☐ _____

☐ _____

☐ _____

Name: _____ Date: _____

Focus on State
Social Awareness

Knowing Your Strengths

Your state is a unique place. Since you live there, you likely know a lot of fun things to do and see. This is something you can share with others when they move to your state to help them feel welcome.

Directions: Imagine a new kid has just moved to your state. List three places you would show them and why you think each place is important.

1. _____

_____

_____

2. _____

_____

_____

3. _____

_____

_____

Directions: Draw one of the places you listed.

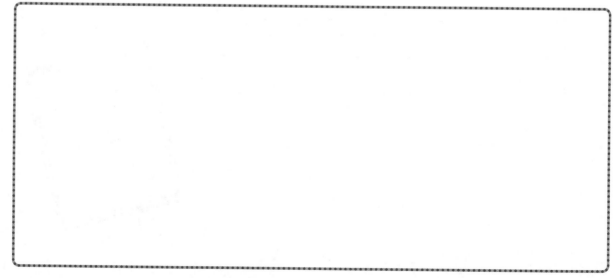

Name: _____ Date: _____

Effective Communication

Being able to communicate is a skill that you can improve with practice and some focus. Be thoughtful about how you communicate. Think clearly about your message. Know to whom you are speaking. This will help you communicate effectively.

Each year, the governor of your state gives a speech called the State of the State. This speech shares how things are going and the governor's plans for the next year. The way this speech is communicated is very important. Governors spend a lot of time thinking about their messages and their audiences. The speech is often communicated in many ways, such as TV, radio, newspaper, and through social media. This helps more people hear and understand their messages.

Directions: Read the information about an event in your neighborhood. Think about how you could communicate this message. List a few options.

Sender of the Message: You

Event: Tenth Annual Neighborhood Picnic

When: July 23 at 1:00 p.m.

What: Bring a dish to share. Be ready to have fun!

_____

_____

Directions: Choose one of your communication methods. Draw what it would look like.

Name: _____ Date: _____

Focus on State

Responsible Decision-Making

Identifying Big and Small Problems

Determining the size of a problem can help you decide whether you need help solving it. To solve big problems, you need help from an adult. Small problems can be solved on your own.

Just like you, your state has problems. Some problems are smaller and can be solved by individual people. Some are bigger and require people to team up to solve them.

Directions: List big and small state problems in the correct boxes. Look at the example in each box to get started.

Small Problems

trash in a state park

Big Problems

broken water line flooded a highway

Honesty and Integrity

Being honest means you tell the truth. Having integrity means doing what you think is right. Both are skills that can be practiced. Most people like to vote for candidates who practice honesty and integrity. So, if you start now, there's no telling where these skills can take you.

Directions: Answer the questions.

1. Describe a time when it was hard to be honest.

_____

_____

_____

2. Why was it hard to be honest?

_____

_____

_____

3. Why is it important to always be honest?

_____

_____

_____

4. What could happen if you are not honest with your friends and family?

_____

_____

_____

Name: _____ Date: _____

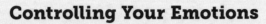

Controlling Your Emotions

Your emotions can get so strong that it might be hard to control them sometimes. If you start feeling big emotions, it is helpful to have a few skills to calm your body down.

Leaders, such as the president and lawmakers, have very stressful jobs. There is so much important work to do. Even leaders need to practice controlling their emotions.

Directions: List calming skills that would fit each of the situations below.

1. Write something you could do quietly in your chair.

_____

_____

2. Write something you could do if you had a five-minute break.

_____

_____

3. Write something you could do if you had 15 minutes to yourself.

_____

_____

. . . .

Directions: Choose one of the things you listed that would work for you right now. Practice it. Then, write how you feel afterwards.

_____

_____

_____

_____

_____

126961—180 Days of Social-Emotional Learning

Name: _____ Date: _____

Someone Else's Perspective

People have different opinions, and that's okay. It is important to still be kind to everyone, even when people think differently than we do. One way to work on that is to think about their point of view. This is also called their *perspective*.

Directions: Read the text. Create a comic strip with pictures and dialogue showing a conversation between you and your parent. Show your parent explaining why they don't want you to walk to your friend's house.

Stormy Weather

Imagine your parent has just told you that you will not be allowed to walk to your friend's house. They tell you that there is a big storm coming, and they don't think it is safe for you to be outside alone. You are very upset, and you think your parent is not being fair.

Focus on Country

Social Awareness

Name: _____ Date: _____

Being a Leader

Our nation's leaders are very important. They inspire us to do our best, and they try to make good decisions for the country.

Directions: Choose a leader from the list, or choose a different U.S. leader you know. Write them a letter about why you appreciate them.

U.S. Leaders

diplomat

president

representative

senator

vice president

_____

_____

_____

_____

_____

_____

_____

_____

_____

_____

_____

_____

_____

Name: _____ **Date:** _____

Making Safe Choices

Making good choices will help keep you safe. You can help set an example for others by making safe choices.

Directions: Write the activities from the box in the correct columns.

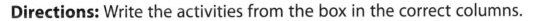

Safe Choices	Unsafe Choices

jaywalking

driving the speed limit

having a neighborhood safety plan

riding in a car without a seatbelt

checking the batteries in a smoke detector

petting a strange dog

using a crosswalk

Name: _____ Date: _____

Discover What You Like

What are you passionate about? What motivates you? Sometimes, we know what our goals are and how to move forward with our passions. Other times, we need to sit back and think about what makes us excited.

Directions: Make a vision board to display things that you like and that motivate you. Your vision board represents you! You can draw pictures, write words, or cut pictures out of a magazine.

Vision Board

© Shell Education

Name: _____ Date: _____

Positive Self-Talk

Sometimes, life gets tough. You just feel out of sorts. When you are feeling low, affirmations can help pull you back up. An affirmation is a positive statement that you say to yourself. It motivates you to keep going. Here are some examples.

Affirmations

I am smart.

I can do hard things.

I am a kind person.

I am loved by my friends and family.

Directions: Write three affirmations that could help when you feel down.

1. _____

2. _____

3. _____

Directions: Write your favorite affirmation in the box. Decorate the words to make your affirmation bright and exciting.

Name: _____ **Date:** _____

Focus on Self

Social Awareness

Gratitude

Being grateful means that you are thankful for the good things in your life. When you think about the positive things you have, you will feel more positive overall. Being grateful can even make you feel physically healthier.

Directions: Start a gratitude journal. List as many things you are grateful for as you can. Write something new every day. Try not to repeat any items if you can.

Day 1 _____

_____

_____

Day 2 _____

_____

_____

Day 3 _____

_____

_____

Day 4 _____

_____

_____

Day 5 _____

_____

_____

Name: _____ Date: _____

Making Good Friends

It is often said that to have good friends, you need to be a good friend. Being a good friend means that you are kind, supportive, and trustworthy. Being a good friend feels good and helps you make even more friends.

Focus on Self
Relationship Skills

Directions: Write the letters of your name vertically. Then, think of a word that matches each letter and describes how you are a good friend. Follow the example.

J–joyful

O–openminded

H–honest

N–nice

Name: _____ Date: _____

Focus on Self

Responsible Decision-Making

Helping Your Community

You might think that role models have to be adults. But you can be a role model for your classmates, siblings, friends, and even adults.

Directions: Draw yourself. Write words around you that show why you are a good role model.

Directions: Describe a situation where you could be a role model for others.

_____

_____

_____

_____

Name: _____ **Date:** _____

Know Your Role Model

Role models are people who will do the right thing. They inspire you to be your best. Family members are often role models. If you are struggling with how to handle a problem, think about what your role model would do.

Directions: Write the name of a family member who is a role model for you. Write what your role model would do in each situation.

Role Model: _____

1. You are playing at the park, and you see a kid getting teased. You want to go help, but you are nervous that the kids will start teasing you, too.

   _____

   _____

   _____

   _____

2. You just had a fight with your brother. You are feeling really angry. You walk into the living room and see that your brother left his social media account open. You want to post something embarrassing.

   _____

   _____

   _____

   _____

3. Your sister complains that your brother is always taking her things without asking. You see your sister's phone in your brother's room.

   _____

   _____

   _____

   _____

Name: _____ Date: _____

Trying Something New

It can be scary to try something new. You can convince yourself that you do not really want to try something. But you may actually just be afraid to fail.

Directions: Finish the sentence three different ways. Then, draw yourself trying one of those things.

If I knew I wouldn't fail, I would…

- _____

- _____

- _____

Directions: Imagine your sibling is scared to try something new. They are worried they will fail if they try. Write three things you could say to them to help them be brave and take a risk.

- _____

- _____

- _____

Focus on Family
Self-Management

The Feelings of Others

It feels good when people say kind things or treat us nicely. You can help others by being kind to them.

One way to think about being kind to someone is to imagine them with a bucket. Are you doing things that will fill their bucket? Or are you emptying their bucket?

Directions: Write the names of three family members on the fronts of the buckets. Then, write five things you could say or do for each person to fill their bucket.

Focus on Family
Social Awareness

Name: _____ Date: _____

Solving Conflicts

Conflicts happen in every family. It can help to practice solving conflicts. This will help you know what to do when they happen in your family.

Remember that conflict solutions can fall into three categories:

Win-Win: Everyone is happy with the solution.

Win-Lose: Only one person is happy with the solution.

Lose-Lose: Everyone is unhappy with the solution.

Directions: Read the text. Write three solutions for the Vasquez family.

The Stained Shirt

Jackie is at home with her sister, Monica. Monica just found out that Jackie wore her clothes to school and there is a stain on her favorite shirt. Monica is angry and wants Jackie to buy her a new shirt. Jackie feels bad, but she does not have the money to buy a new shirt.

1. Win-Win Solution

_____

_____

_____

2. Win-Lose Solution

_____

_____

_____

3. Lose-Lose Solution

_____

_____

_____

Name: _____ **Date:** _____

Consequences of My Actions

Your actions have consequences. This means the things you do can make people feel good, or they can make people feel bad. It's important to think about this and take responsibility for your actions.

Directions: Write how your actions would make someone feel in each situation.

1. You are playing a board game with your cousin. You unexpectedly come from behind and win. You jump up and start cheering while teasing your cousin.

   _____

   _____

   _____

2. You know your parent is working really long hours right now. They are always very tired. You want to do something nice for them, so you get up after everyone has gone to bed and pack them a lunch for the next day. You leave a note in the lunch, telling them to have a great day.

   _____

   _____

   _____

3. Describe an interaction between you and a family member that ended with good or bad feelings.

   _____

   _____

   _____

   _____

Name: _____ Date: _____

Identifying Your Emotions

Something in your community will impact your emotions every day. Knowing this will help you deal with those feelings.

Directions: Write how each situation would make the person feel.

1. There is a block party in Lisa's community. When she gets to the party, she learns that there are ponies to ride. Lisa has always wanted to ride a pony!

_____

_____

_____

2. When Samuel arrives at his favorite bakery, it is closed. He is really confused. The bakery is always open. Samuel soon finds out that the elderly man who runs the bakery has passed away.

_____

_____

_____

3. Daniel is walking to his grandma's house. On the way, he sees that an empty building is being turned into an ice cream shop.

_____

_____

_____

4. On her way to school, Hazel sees that the windows are boarded up in a store. When she gets to school, a friend tells her that the store was robbed.

_____

_____

_____

Name: _____ Date: _____

Controlling Your Emotions

It is normal to have big feelings. Sometimes, people do not realize how big their feelings are until they are ready to burst. Knowing when your feelings are growing can help you calm yourself before they get too big.

Directions: Order the feelings in the box from the least intense to the most intense. Then, write how each emotion makes your body feel.

angry   frustrated

annoyed   furious

calm

Most Intense

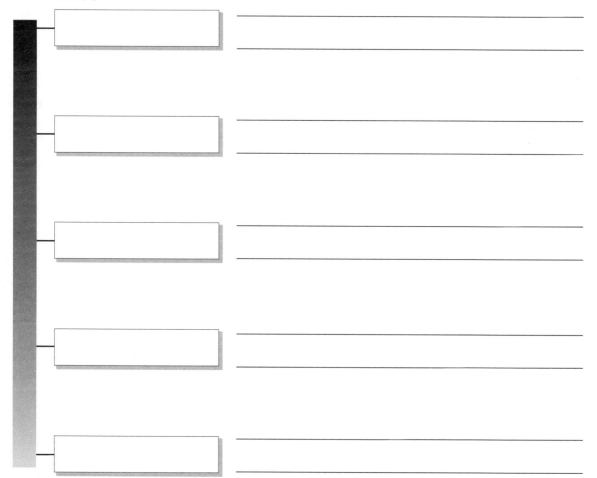

Least Intense

Name: _____ Date: _____

Focus on Community
Social Awareness

The Feelings of Others

Thinking about the feelings of others will help you know if you can help. You may be able to help someone feel better.

Directions: Write how the person in each picture might be feeling. Then, write something you could do to help.

1. How is this person feeling? _____

2. What could you help them feel better?

   _____

   _____

   _____

3. How is this person feeling? _____

4. What could you help them feel better?

   _____

   _____

   _____

Directions: Draw someone with a strong feeling.

Working as a Team

Sometimes, things are hard to do on your own. But when you work as a team, you can get things done faster and have fun along the way.

Directions: Read the scenario. Write your plan to fix the ball field. Include yourself and three people in your community who can help. Assign each person a task.

Baseball Field

You and your friends are getting ready to play your first baseball game of the year. But the field is in bad shape. There are puddles of water, a missing base, leaves on the infield, and broken benches. The field needs to get fixed before you can play, but it is too much to do on your own. You and your friends need a plan to get it fixed.

1. _____

_____

2. _____

_____

3. _____

_____

4. _____

_____

Focus on Community

Relationship Skills

Name: _____ Date: _____

Helping Your Community

Your community is a special place. It is your home and where you are growing up. You can help your community by helping to keep it a safe and special place to live.

Directions: Describe something special you could do to give back to your community. What would you do if you had all the money and support you wanted? Think big! Then, draw what you would do.

_____

_____

_____

_____

Name: _____ **Date:** _____

Feelings, Thoughts, and Values

You have a lot of thoughts and feelings every day. Being able to understand how you are feeling will help you understand your values. Your values are the things that are most important to you.

A motto is a phrase or saying that shows a person's or organization's values or beliefs. The motto for the Olympics is "Faster, Higher, Stronger." States also have mottos. Alaska's motto is "North to the Future."

Directions: Write your motto. It should be short and show your values or beliefs. Then, draw a picture showing your values or beliefs.

Name: _____ Date: _____

Managing Your Emotions

It can be tough to manage your emotions when you are really nervous. It is also hard to make decisions at that time. Knowing how to calm your mind will help you return to a calm place where you can make good decisions.

Focus on State

Self-Management

Directions: Read the scenarios, and answer the questions.

1. You are playing in your state basketball championship game. You are really nervous. The pressure and anxiety are making it hard for you to make clear decisions. There is a 20-second time-out. Describe how you could calm your mind.

   _____

   _____

   _____

2. You are calm and back on the court. Now, you need to get through the rest of the game. Write some self-talk you can use to stay focused.

   _____

   _____

   _____

3. How can you calm your mind in your daily life?

   _____

   _____

   _____

   _____

Name: _____ **Date:** _____

Showing Gratitude

Being grateful to others feels good. But it's easy to forget to notice all the things that you have to be grateful for.

Directions: Think of someone who works hard to keep your state safe and healthy. It could be a park ranger, a social worker, the governor, a state trooper, a teacher, or someone else. Draw a comic to show how grateful you are for their work. Show how it makes your community better.

Name: _____ Date: _____

Developing Positive Relationships

Friends help us get through the tough parts of life. They also celebrate with us when we are happy. Having good friends not only feels good, but it can also make you healthier.

Focus on State

Relationship Skills

Directions: Write a letter to a friend. Tell them how thankful you are for their friendship. Write about what you enjoy doing together and what you want to do together in the future.

_____

_____

_____

_____

_____

_____

_____

_____

_____

_____

_____

_____

_____

_____

_____

_____

                                    _____

                                    _____

126961—180 Days of Social-Emotional Learning

Name: _____ Date: _____

Identifying Solutions to Problems

Even really big problems have solutions. We just have to be willing to find them. You can help find solutions to a problem by being thoughtful and creative. Sometimes, your solution will not work, and that's okay. You just have to try again.

Directions: Map out a solution to this conflict using the flow chart.

You open your social media account and find that your friend has posted a picture of you that you do not like. Your friend does not want to take the picture down.

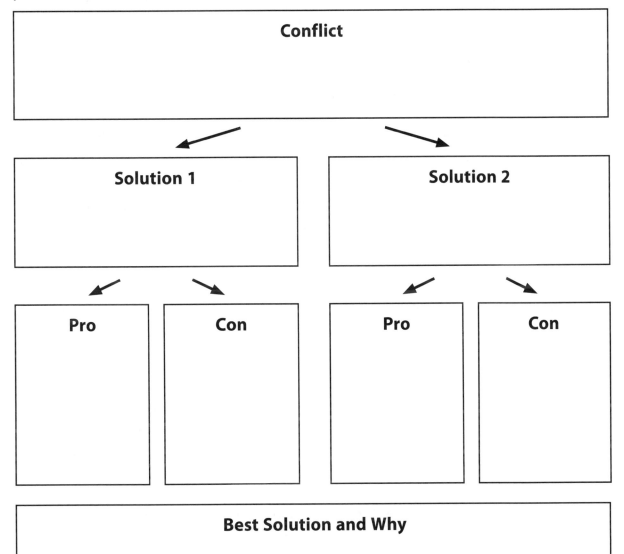

Conflict

Solution 1	**Solution 2**

Pro	**Con**	**Pro**	**Con**

Best Solution and Why

Name: _____ Date: _____

Focus on Country

Self-Awareness

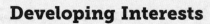

Developing Interests

Being open-minded could help you find a new passion. You never know until you try something if it will be something you really love.

Directions: Study the list of activities. Then, rank your five favorites. Write *1* next to the activity you most want to try. Write *2* next to your next favorite, and so on. You will have activities left over.

acting	ice skating
building a computer	painting
cake decorating	playing a new sport
cooking	singing
driving a race car	skydiving
flying a plane	traveling to another country

Directions: Choose one activity you numbered that you could do now. Explain why it is something you want to try. Then, draw yourself doing it.

_____

_____

Name: _____ **Date:** _____

Being Brave

Being brave can be scary. But it can also mean doing something new and exciting. It doesn't have to be something big. Even small steps take bravery.

Jackie Robinson did something brave and new when he joined the Brooklyn Dodgers. He was the first Black player in Major League Baseball. It was very hard for Jackie Robinson. Some players and fans were not kind to him. But Robinson stuck with it. He became MVP in 1949. He led the way for other Black athletes.

Directions: Write a short story about someone trying something new. Explain their emotions. Describe the outcome.

_____

_____

_____

_____

_____

_____

_____

_____

_____

_____

_____

_____

_____

_____

_____

_____

_____

Focus on Country

Self-Management

Name: _____ Date: _____

Focus on Country

Social Awareness

Seeing Strengths in Others

Everyone has strengths. Sometimes, it is hard for people to see their own strengths. They may need someone else to help point them out.

Coaches think about who will fill each position. They consider the strengths of each individual and how they will work as a team.

Directions: Imagine you are a soccer coach of a team that is going to the Olympics. You have a few open positions to fill. Consider the strengths of the people you know. Fill each position. Explain why you chose each person.

1. Goalie: _____

_____

_____

2. Assistant Coach: _____

_____

_____

3. Team Doctor: _____

_____

_____

4. Team Captain: _____

_____

_____

Name: _____ **Date:** _____

Being a Leader

Leaders are not all alike. They can lead by doing a lot of different things. Successful leaders lead in a way that helps people feel good about what they are doing. They also inspire people to do more.

Ruth Bader Ginsburg was an Associate Justice for the Supreme Court. She was known for her willingness to be honest and fight for others. Ginsburg once said, "Fight for the things that you care about. But do it in a way that will lead others to join you."

Directions: Imagine you are the captain of a hockey team that is in a close playoff game. But your team is struggling. It is the end of the second period, and your team is behind. What could you say to inspire and motivate them?

_____

_____

_____

_____

_____

Directions: Write how you can be a leader in your daily life.

_____

_____

_____

_____

_____

Focus on Country

Relationship Skills

Name: _____ Date: _____

Your Actions Impact Others

Your actions can impact others. Think about throwing a rock into a lake. Little ripples radiate from the point where the rock entered the water. The ripples are like your actions. They stay around long after the rock is gone and affect other parts of the lake.

Neil Armstrong was the first person to walk on the moon. This was important not only for Americans, but also for people around the world. Walking on the moon seemed impossible. By showing that it could be done, Armstrong inspired others to conquer their own dreams.

Directions: Describe something that you have always wanted to do. Then, draw yourself achieving it.

_____

_____

_____

Identifying Personal Assets

You are an individual. But you are also a citizen of the world. That means you matter to the world, and you can use your skills to make the world a better place. Even small actions can have a big impact.

Directions: Describe three skills you have that could make the world a better place. Circle one of your skills. Draw yourself using the skill to help others.

1. _____

2. _____

3. _____

Focus on World
Self-Awareness

Name: _____ Date: _____

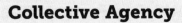

Collective Agency

We can do a lot when we work together. *Collective agency* is when people come together for a common cause. When people do this, they can achieve goals that would otherwise seem impossible.

One of the world's greatest achievements is the International Space Station. Fifteen countries worked as a group to build it. Since 2011, those countries have helped us learn more about space and the world.

Directions: Describe something you were able to accomplish because you worked with a group. Who helped? What did you accomplish? How did you work together? Then, draw your accomplishment.

_____

_____

_____

_____

Name: _____ **Date:** _____

The Influence of Systems

A *system* is something that can have a positive influence on our lives. It can help us make good decisions. It can help make the world better for everyone.

One example of a system is the phrase "Reduce, Reuse, Recycle." The system was created in the 1970s to help people make good decisions. It has led to less waste and less pollution around the world.

Directions: Draw things you do to reduce, reuse, and recycle.

Focus on World
Social Awareness

Name: _____ Date: _____

Focus on World

Relationship Skills

Collaborative Problem-Solving

Problems can be too big to solve alone. *Collaborative problem-solving* is when a group of people solve a problem together. They can solve the problem quicker. They can also come up with a better answer.

One of the largest groups that does this is the United Nations. It is committed to world peace and protecting human rights. Countries know they can do much more good together than they could do alone.

Directions: Read the text. Write a collaborative solution to this problem.

Class Pet

Loretta and Sandi are feeding the class hamster when the cage door slips open. The hamster escapes. The hamster runs behind a bookshelf and will not come out. Loretta and Sandi know that the hamster likes carrots and is really fast. The bookshelf is also very heavy. They have many friends nearby to help.

_____

_____

_____

_____

_____

_____

_____

_____

_____

_____

_____

Solutions for Social Problems

You have the skills to solve problems. You can solve problems for yourself. You can also think about social problems in your community or school and find those solutions, too.

Rotary International is a group that works on big problems. In 1979, it took on a huge problem. Rotary saw that many children still got polio. Polio is a disease that can paralyze children. But there is a vaccine that prevents it. Rotary gave the vaccine to as many children as possible. Now, polio is almost totally gone.

Focus on World

Responsible Decision-Making

Directions: Write three creative solutions for each problem.

1. Your class is supposed to be going on a field trip. But you just found out the bus is broken. How else could you get to the field trip?

_____

_____

_____

_____

_____

_____

2. The basketball court in your neighborhood has been damaged in a storm. One of the hoops is broken. Everyone wants to play basketball this weekend. What could you do to make sure everyone gets to play?

_____

_____

_____

_____

Answer Key

There are many open-ended questions and writing prompts in this book. For those activities, the answers will vary. Examples are given as needed.

Week 1 Day 1 (page 12)

Joy—thrilled, happy, content, cheerful, delighted

Anger—furious, raging, mad, exasperated, fuming

Fear—frightful, terrified, panicked, horrified

Disgust—repulsed, sickened

Sadness—concerned, depressed, upset, devastated, miserable

Week 1 Day 3 (page 14)

1. happy
2. scared
3. sad
4. frustrated

Week 1 Day 5 (page 16)

1. small problem
2. big problem
3. small problem
4. big problem

Week 2 Day 2 (page 18)

Examples:

1. I will get a cell phone someday. My parents are just trying to look out for me. Maybe my friend will let me use her phone sometimes.
2. I am so bummed, but at least I can talk to them on the phone. I know I will get to see them again soon.

Week 2 Day 3 (page 19)

1. angry, annoyed, or frustrated
2. She bangs Joey's leg and mutters under her breath for him to move.
3. angry, annoyed, or frustrated
4. He rolls his eyes, shouts at Sara, and doesn't want to move.

Week 2 Day 4 (page 20)

1. Sender: Elena; Receiver: Luis; Message: plot of a book
2. Sender: Shawn; Receiver: Shawn's mom; Message: It's unfair to make him stay home
3. Sender: Monique's grandma; Receiver: Monique; Message: grandma planted vegetables

Week 3 Day 4 (page 25)

Examples:

1. She could introduce herself and ask if she could warm up with them.
2. He could compliment their bikes and ask them about their bikes.
3. She could ask to sit next to the kid from her science class.

Week 4 Day 1 (page 27)

1. Maria would be able to read the labels.
2. Andrew would be able to help the lost people find their way.

Week 6 Day 5 (page 41)

Examples:

1. **Overreaction:** They're probably saying bad things about me.
   Appropriate Reaction: I don't know what they're saying. Maybe it's something good.
2. **Overreaction:** He must not like me anymore.
   Appropriate Reaction: Maybe he made a new friend and will sit with me tomorrow.
3. **Overreaction:** She never listens to me! She did this on purpose.
   Appropriate Reaction: I'm frustrated that she didn't listen to me. I'll remind her that I didn't want her to touch it.
4. **Overreaction:** My coach doesn't think I'm any good.
   Appropriate Reaction: Maybe my coach thinks I need a break.

Week 7 Day 3 (page 44)

Examples:

1. Friend: "I failed my test! I am in so much trouble!"
   You: "I'm sorry. Maybe if you explain to your parents what went wrong, they will understand."
2. Friend: "Jane has been making fun of me, and I am really upset."
   You: "That's not nice. I will be here for you."

Answer Key *(cont.)*

Week 7 Day 4 (page 45)

Good Communication: asking questions when a person is done talking; making eye contact; speaking clearly

Poor Communication: assuming you know what a person will say; crossing your arms; looking down at the floor

Week 8 Day 1 (page 47)

1. The boys broke the car window.
2. They would not tell Mr. Salvador what happened.
3. They would tell Mr. Salvador what happened and ask how to fix their mistake.
4. Example: I would tell Mr. Salvador what happened. I would ask a parent to go with me.

Week 8 Day 5 (page 51)

Library: loans books, holds story time, has computers for people to use, safe place to spend time

Shelter: feeds the hungry, offers resources and support to those in need

School: teaches students, gives students meals, safe place for students to go

Fire Station: puts out fires, helps in medical emergencies

Week 9 Day 3 (page 54)

1. Drive the speed limit.
2. Buckle their seatbelt.
3. Put the trash in a trash can.
4. Use the crosswalk to cross the street.
5. Example: People have to act safely, or else they will have to pay fines or go to jail.
6. Example: You have to buckle your seatbelt in a car.

Week 9 Day 5 (page 56)

1. *A big campfire* leads to *smoke in the sky* which leads to *air pollution.*
2. *Eating healthy food* leads to *a healthier body* which leads to *more energy.*

Week 10 Day 3 (page 59)

The first and last pictures should be circled.
Examples:

1. Let boys and girls play together.
2. Meet on the first floor.

Week 11 Day 3 (page 64)

Examples:

1. Frustrated that I did not take care of their sweatshirt.
2. They would probably not let me borrow anything.
3. Angry that I told their secret.
4. They would probably not tell me the secret.
5. Happy and supported because I stood up for them.
6. They might stick up for me if someone were teasing me.

Week 11 Day 4 (page 65)

Examples:

1. I feel frustrated when you don't help me. Next time, I will wait until you can help me so we can do this together.
2. I feel angry when you interrupt me while I am trying to read the instructions. Next time, can you please wait until I am done reading to talk to me?
3. Julia could start building with Kent to get it going and then read the directions while Kent continues to build.

Week 11 Day 5 (page 66)

Examples:

1. Two activities occur at the same time.
2. I could quit basketball and try out for band.
3. I might miss basketball. My team would lose a player.
4. My friend wants to take the money.
5. We take the wallet.
6. We feel horrible. The person loses their money and identification.

Week 12 Day 1 (page 67)

Growth Mindset: I am struggling with math. I know I can get better if I try; If I stay calm and focus, I will be able to figure out this problem; I am feeling really angry right now. When I wake up tomorrow, things will seem better.

Fixed Mindset: I am never going to make a new friend. I am going to be alone forever; This test is so hard. I am going to fail no matter what; I hate running. I am never going to get faster.

Answer Key *(cont.)*

Week 12 Day 3 (page 69)

Examples:

1. Lucy needs help with math. She needs help studying for the test. Lucy also needs a plan to get caught up with her assignments.
2. Lucy could ask a teacher or friend or get a tutor to help.
3. Kamaar needs a plan to handle the people teasing him.
4. Kamaar could ask a friend, teacher, parent, or a school counselor for help.

Week 12 Day 4 (page 70)

Examples:

1. Tell the person firmly that everyone needs to contribute to the project.
2. Tell the kids that it is not kind to make fun of other people.

Week 13 Day 1 (page 72)

Examples:

Someone breaks the basketball hoop at your local park—you feel angry—you kick a basketball over the fence.

You see a neighbor drop litter on the side of the street—you feel disappointed—you make a sign that says Be Kind to Earth, Don't Litter.

Week 13 Day 4 (page 75)

Top: Lose-Lose

Middle: Win-Lose

Bottom: Win-Win

Examples:

Win-Win: We could buy the candy together and split it.

Win-Lose: I could buy the candy and not share.

Lose-Lose: No one could buy the candy.

Week 13 Day 5 (page 76)

Examples:

1. Walk with the woman to keep her company and help her get home safe.
2. Ask an adult to help them find their way.
3. Organize a litter pickup in your community.
4. Get a shovel, and help clear the snow.

Week 14 Day 1 (page 77)

1. Tony has a bias.
2. The person who cast the play has a bias.

Week 14 Day 2 (page 78)

1. The goal was to get the medicine to Nome.
2. The dog teams and their mushers got the medicine to Nome.
3. They would probably not have been successful in getting the medicine to the town.

Week 14 Day 3 (page 79)

1. fair; Everyone is safer on the roads.
2. unfair; Boys should be able to play, too.
3. fair; Places are cleaner for everyone.
4. fair; That keeps everyone safer in the park.

Week 14 Day 4 (page 80)

1. She is helping the woman onto the sidewalk safely.
2. She is helping by pushing another kid on the swing.
3. They are helping pick up trash.
4. He is helping to fix another kid's bike.

Week 15 Day 2 (page 83)

1. Example: I'm having a hard time learning to ride my bike. I can get better if I practice.
2. positive self-talk
3. positive self-talk
4. Example: I need to write myself a note so I remember next time.
5. Example: I know I can do better if I calm down and practice.
6. positive self-talk

Week 15 Day 3 (page 84)

Examples:

1. We need houses and books and paper to use for school. Trees make all of these things, so we should cut down trees to make the things we need.
2. We need trees to give us oxygen and to provide homes for animals. We should protect our forests and not cut them down.
3. Trees are very important. Some trees need to be cut down, and some trees need to be preserved.

Answer Key *(cont.)*

Week 16 Day 1 (page 87)

Examples:

1. Copying the essay would be called plagiarism. It is wrong to copy someone else's work and claim it as your own.
2. My teacher might realize I copied the essay and give me an F.
3. Even if you can't see the other people online, they are still real people who deserve to be treated fairly and honestly.

Week 16 Day 2 (page 88)

Examples:

1. Set timers or use programs that track my time.
2. Set limits on when or where to use my device. Keep my device only in the living room. Don't go online until homework is done.
3. go on a walk, talk to a friend, play a game

Week 16 Day 3 (page 89)

Examples:

1. Don't give out your personal information.
2. Only go to websites that are safe.
3. Check with guardians before you buy anything online.
4. Do not meet up in person with people you meet online.
5. Don't say something online you wouldn't say to someone's face.
6. Set strong passwords.

Week 16 Day 4 (page 90)

1. laugh out loud
2. be right back
3. talk to you later
4. I don't know
5. They are yelling at you.
6. Autocorrect has made the message confusing. They meant "Can I come over to your house?"

Week 16 Day 5 (page 91)

Examples:

1. Your parents could find out and punish you. You will break their trust.
2. You could embarrass them and make them feel bad.
3. They could be a dangerous person who now knows where you live.

Week 17 Day 1 (page 92)

1. She tells her mom the truth about the broken vase.
2. Naomi will feel good and maintain her mom's trust.
3. She tells her mom the dog broke the vase.
4. Naomi would feel guilty, her mom could find out, and her trust would be broken.

Week 18 Day 1 (page 97)

1. The pizza company might be prejudiced against people who have disabilities.
2. They did not hire Sharissa for a job.
3. They don't think girls can play baseball.
4. Example: He could stick up for her and ask if she wants to play for his team.

Week 18 Day 2 (page 98)

Examples:

1. Say something encouraging, such as, "You will get it next time."
2. Go sit with them and talk to them.

Week 18 Day 3 (page 99)

1. False
2. True
3. True
4. False

Week 18 Day 4 (page 100)

Examples:

1. "I hear that it scared you when you were alone. We can walk home together, okay?"
2. "I will try this on my own and ask my neighbor if I don't get it. If that doesn't work, I can come back to you, right?"

Week 18 Day 5 (page 101)

1. The noise from the construction is keeping people awake.
2. They want to shut down the construction.
3. They want to get their job done as soon as possible.
4. Examples: agreeing upon different work hours, adjusting work hours for the weekend, doing loud tasks during the middle of the day.

Answer Key *(cont.)*

Week 19 Day 2 (page 103)

Examples:

1. one week

2. my parents, my friends, and their parents

3. tools, wood, shovels, sand bags, trash bags

4. bad weather, missing supplies, people getting busy

5. plan for another day, send someone to a different store, find other people to help

6. The park will be ready for visitors to play again.

Week 20 Day 1 (page 107)

Examples:

1. Christina can talk to a teacher or ask her family for help. Or she can ask another classmate to help her understand the material.

2. Max can go find a teacher or talk to his parents and tell them he needs help. He can also make a friend to have as a buddy who could help him at recess. Max could learn some things to say to firmly stand up for himself.

Week 20 Day 3 (page 109)

Examples:

1. Rhonda is feeling really sad and maybe jealous or annoyed that Tina made the team. Tina could tell her how great she did and that it's okay to be sad that she didn't make the team.

2. The other candidates are feeling sad and frustrated. They might feel jealous or annoyed that Juan won. He can be a gracious winner and not make them feel bad about it.

3. Marcy is feeling disappointed and frustrated. Terry could tell her that he's sorry things didn't work out the way she wanted and remind her that she'll get to vote again in four years.

4. Liam is disappointed and frustrated that his project didn't work. Jordan could be a gracious winner. She could compliment his effort and his ideas.

Week 21 Day 5 (page 116)

Examples:

1. I feel embarrassed, but everyone makes mistakes. I am going to see if they are okay.

2. I am really sorry I pushed you down. I got really into the game and didn't realize how rough I was being. Are you okay? I will tone it down a bit.

3. I didn't mean to damage the book. My friend will forgive me if I apologize and try to make things right.

4. I am really sorry about your book. I should have kept it away from my dog. Let me talk to our teacher and see what I can do to fix this.

Week 22 Day 2 (page 118)

Examples:

1. angry, frustrated

2. He might be less upset.

3. She might feel good about the game and want to play with him again.

4. He might feel disappointed in his actions.

5. She might feel sad, disappointed. She might not want to play with him anymore.

6. Cassie could say, "Wow, you almost had me! That was fun!"

Week 24 Day 3 (page 129)

Examples:

Pros: It will keep people safe; it will keep people focused on the road; people will not be distracted; people will keep two hands on the wheel; there will be fewer accidents.

Cons: Handsfree features make talking safe; sometimes things come up, and you need to answer a call; it can be helpful to use maps to get where you are going; most cars are programmed to talk to phones more safely; law enforcement need to use their devices.

Week 24 Day 4 (page 130)

Examples:

1. I feel really nervous about school. In the summer, I need a break.

2. Tell me why you want to go to school in the summer. I'd love to hear your reasons!

3. I'm not sure I agree. I like my summer break. Why do you think that would be a good idea?

Answer Key *(cont.)*

Week 25 Day 1 (page 132)

1. Give the wallet to the man who lost it.
2. Jamal would feel guilty if he kept the money, but he would be happy to have money to buy snacks.
3. Jamal would feel good for giving the wallet back, but he might feel bad if his friend was mad at him.
4. Example: Jamal could tell Zach that it is the right thing to do to give the wallet back.

Week 26 Day 2 (page 138)

Helpful Coping Skills: count to 10; draw a picture; positive self-talk; read a book; take a break; take a deep breath; take a walk; talk to a friend

Not Helpful Coping Skills: punch a wall; roll your eyes; scream; slam a door; storm off; sulk; throw things

Week 26 Day 3 (page 139)

1. upset, concerned
2. sad
3. happy, in love

Week 27 Day 1 (page 142)

Examples:

1. Math is hard for me, but with some work I can figure it out.
2. My art is beautiful, even if it is different from other people's art.
3. I am a good friend, and I am going to meet someone awesome.
4. With some extra practice, I can get better at basketball.
5. Everyone starts on the easier slopes. I'll get it!
6. I can become a great player if I practice every day.

Week 27 Day 3 (page 144)

Examples:

1. I could ask the kid to play with me and my friends.
2. I could pass the ball to them first.
3. I could tell other kids to stop teasing her.
4. I could ask the boy what he does like.
5. I could make sure to include that kid.
6. I could invite them to sit with my friends.

Week 27 Day 4 (page 145)

Examples:

1. No, I won't do that. I'm so sorry you forgot to do your homework. I want to keep my work my own.
2. I can't do that. I made a promise to my parents, and I want to keep their trust.

Week 27 Day 5 (page 146)

Examples:

1. I could suggest that they split the time in half and each read the book they want for half the reading time.
2. I could ask the kid who kicked the ball to apologize and tell the injured kid that it was an accident. Then, I could get him ice or something to make it better.

Week 28 Day 3 (page 149)

Examples:

Good: Veronica could love acting in a play; Veronica could meet new friends; Veronica could find another part of theatre that she likes; Veronica might be proud of herself for trying something new

Bad: Veronica could not like acting in a play; Veronica could not like being in front of people

Week 28 Day 5 (page 151)

Examples: get to know my neighbors so I know who lives near me; know the numbers to contact police or other help; let an adult know right away if I see something that looks dangerous

Week 29 Day 5 (page 156)

Examples:

Small Problems: broken basketball court; graffiti on the wall; burned-out streetlights

Big Problems: broken water pipe, fallen powerline, big potholes in the road

Week 30 Day 1 (page 157)

2. It can be hard to be honest because sometimes the truth is embarrassing.
3. Honesty builds trust with others. People know they can count on you. It helps your friendships when people know you are trustworthy.
4. When you are not honest, people learn they can't trust you. This can break down relationships.

Week 30 Day 2 (page 158)

Examples:

1. take deep breaths
2. close my eyes and check in with my body
3. take a walk

Answer Key *(cont.)*

Week 30 Day 5 (page 161)

Safe Choices: checking the batteries in a smoke detector; driving the speed limit; having a neighborhood safety plan; using a crosswalk

Unsafe Choices: jaywalking; petting a strange dog; riding in a car without a seatbelt

Week 32 Day 4 (page 170)

1. Win-Win—Monica and Jackie work together to come up with a way to earn money to buy the shirt.
2. Win-Lose—Jackie gives Monica one of Jackie's favorite shirts.
3. Lose-Lose—Jackie refuses to do anything to replace the shirt.

Week 32 Day 5 (page 171)

1. sad, frustrated, mad
2. happy, loved, supported

Week 33 Day 1 (page 172)

1. excited, happy, surprised
2. sad, surprised, disappointed
3. excited, happy, surprised
4. scared, nervous, mad

Week 33 Day 2 (page 173)

Examples:

furious: hard to see, headache

angry: clenched fists, upset stomach

frustrated: frowning face, tense muscles

annoyed: furrowed brow, tense muscles

calm: relaxed, smiling

Week 33 Day 3 (page 174)

1. sad
2. I could talk to them or help get them a new ice cream.
3. nervous
4. I could cheer for them and say encouraging things.

Week 36 Day 5 (page 191)

Examples:

1. You could walk to the field trip; You could go to the field trip tomorrow when the bus is fixed; You could use public transportation to get to the field trip; You could do a virtual field trip.
2. You could pull some people together to help fix the hoop; You could find another court to play on; You could play a half-court game.

References Cited

The Aspen Institute: National Commission on Social, Emotional, & Academic Development. 2018. "From a Nation at Risk to a Nation at Hope." https://nationathope.org/wp-content/uploads/2018_aspen_final-report_full_webversion.pdf.

Collaborative for Academic, Social, and Emotional Learning (CASEL). n.d. "What Is SEL?" Last modified December 2020. https://casel.org/what-is-sel/.

Durlak, Joseph A., Roger P. Weissberg, Allison B. Dymnicki, Rebecca D. Taylor, and Kriston B. Schellinger. 2011. "The Impact of Enhancing Students' Social and Emotional Learning: A Meta-Analysis of School-Based Universal Interventions." *Child Development* 82 (1): 405–32.

Goleman, Daniel. 2005. *Emotional Intelligence: Why It Can Matter More Than IQ.* New York: Bantam Dell.

Palmer, Parker J. 2007. *The Courage to Teach: Exploring the Inner Landscape of a Teacher's Life.* San Francisco: Jossey-Bass.

Name: _____ Date: _____

Connecting to Self Rubric

Days 1 and 2

Directions: Complete this rubric every six weeks to evaluate students' Day 1 and Day 2 activity sheets. Only one rubric is needed per student. Their work over the six weeks can be considered together. Appraise their work in each category by circling or highlighting the descriptor in each row that best describes the student's work. Then, consider the student's overall progress in connecting to self. In the box, draw ☆, ✓+ , or ✓ to indicate your overall evaluation.

Competency	Advanced	Satisfactory	Developing
Self-Awareness	Can accurately identify one's own full range of emotions.	Identifies one's own emotions accurately most of the time.	Has trouble identifying their own feelings.
	Understands that thoughts and feelings are connected.	Sees the connection of thoughts and feelings most of the time.	Does not connect thoughts to feelings.
	Can identify strengths and areas of growth.	Can identify a few strengths and weaknesses.	Can identify only one strength or weakness.
Self-Management	Can manage stress by using several different strategies.	Manages stress with only one strategy.	Does not manage stress well.
	Shows motivation in all areas of learning.	Shows motivation in a few areas of learning.	Shows little to no motivation.
	Is able to set realistic goals.	Sets some goals that are realistic and some that are not.	Has a hard time setting goals that are achievable.

Comments

_____

_____

_____

_____

Overall

[ ]

Name: _____ Date: _____

Relating to Others Rubric

Days 3 and 4

Directions: Complete this rubric every six weeks to evaluate students' Day 3 and Day 4 activity sheets. Only one rubric is needed per student. Their work over the six weeks can be considered together. Appraise their work in each category by circling or highlighting the descriptor in each row that best describes the student's work. Then, consider the student's overall progress in relating to others. In the box, draw ☆, ✓+ , or ✓ to indicate your overall evaluation.

Competency	Advanced	Satisfactory	Developing
Social Awareness	Shows empathy toward others.	Shows empathy toward others most of the time.	Shows little to no empathy toward others.
	Can explain how rules are different in different places.	Knows that some places can have different rules.	Is not able to articulate how rules may change in different places.
	Can list many people who support them in their learning.	Can list some people who support them in their learning.	Can list few people who support them in their learning.
Relationship Skills	Uses a variety of strategies to solve conflicts with peers.	Has a few strategies to solve conflicts with peers.	Struggles to solve conflicts with peers.
	Uses advanced skills of listening and paraphrasing while communicating.	Is able to communicate effectively.	Has breakdowns in communication skills.
	Works effectively with a team. Shows leadership in accomplishing team goals.	Works effectively with a team most of the time.	Has trouble working with others on a team.

Comments

Overall

_____

_____

_____

_____

Name: _____ Date: _____

Making Decisions Rubric

Day 5

Directions: Complete this rubric every six weeks to evaluate students' Day 5 activity sheets. Only one rubric is needed per student. Their work over the six weeks can be considered together. Appraise their work in each category by circling or highlighting the descriptor in each row that best describes the student's work. Then, consider the student's overall progress in making decisions. In the box, draw ☆, ✓+ , or ✓ to indicate your overall evaluation.

Competency	Advanced	Satisfactory	Developing
Responsible Decision-Making	Makes decisions that benefit their own long-term interests.	Makes decisions that are sometimes impulsive and sometimes thought out.	Is impulsive and has a hard time making constructive choices.
	Knows how to keep self and others safe in a variety of situations.	Knows how to keep themselves safe in most situations.	Is capable of being safe, but sometimes is not.
	Is able to consider the consequences of their actions, both good and bad.	Is able to identify some consequences of their actions.	Struggles to anticipate possible consequences to their actions.

Comments

_____

_____

_____

_____

Overall

Connecting to Self Analysis

Directions: Record each student's overall symbols (page 200) in the appropriate columns. At a glance, you can view: (1) which students need more help mastering these skills and (2) how students progress throughout the school year.

Student Name	Week 6	Week 12	Week 18	Week 24	Week 30	Week 36

Relating to Others Analysis

Directions: Record each student's overall symbols (page 201) in the appropriate columns. At a glance, you can view: (1) which students need more help mastering these skills and (2) how students progress throughout the school year.

Student Name	Week 6	Week 12	Week 18	Week 24	Week 30	Week 36

Making Decisions Analysis

Directions: Record each student's overall symbols (page 202) in the appropriate columns. At a glance, you can view: (1) which students need more help mastering these skills and (2) how students progress throughout the school year.

Student Name	Week 6	Week 12	Week 18	Week 24	Week 30	Week 36

Digital Resources

Accessing the Digital Resources

The Digital Resources can be downloaded by following these steps:

1. Go to **www.tcmpub.com/digital**

2. Use the ISBN number to redeem the Digital Resources.

3. Respond to the question using the book.

4. Follow the prompts on the Content Cloud website to sign in or create a new account.

5. Choose the Digital Resources you would like to download. You can download all the files at once, or a specific group of files.

ISBN:
9781087649740

Notes

Notes